CANADIAN HOCKEY TRIVIA

The Facts, Stats & Strange Tales of Canadian Hockey

J. Alexander Poulton

OVER TIME BOOKS

The Publisher: OverTime Books is an imprint of Éditions de la Montagne Verte

Library and Archives Canada Cataloguing in Publication

Poulton, J. Alexander (Jay Alexander), 1977–
   Canadian hockey trivia : The facts, stats & strange tales of Canadian hockey / J. Alexander Poulton.

Includes bibliographical references.
ISBN 13: 978-1-897277-01-0
ISBN 10: 1-897277-01-6

   1. Hockey—Canada—Miscellanea. I. Title.

GV848.4.C3P69 2005   796.9620971 C2006-904205-5 GV848.4*

Project Director: J. Alexander Poulton

Cover & Title Page Images: Wayne Gretzky and Eric Lindros. Courtesy of the Hockey Hall of Fame, photo by Paul Bereswill.

PC: P5

Dedication

To my family

Contents

Acknowledgements

I would like to acknowledge all my friends who helped this book along the way. Frank, thanks for question 20. Leo, Naz, Mike, Colin, Liz, Richard, Pete, Gilles, Vahak, Leslie, Vanessa, Zuleika, Nora, and all those I might have forgotten, thanks for all your support. Faye, I could not have completed this without your friendship. Thanks also to all the statisticians who attend every game and mark everything down from the number of shots per player per period per game to the amount of goals and assists: each number, fact and percentage played an important part in the creation of this book.

Introduction

Ever since the first organized game of hockey was played in the late 19th century, the popularity of the sport and people's passion for the game have grown at a steady pace. Since most of us will never get anywhere near playing in the big leagues, we watch every move and record every statistic of the best players in the fastest sport in the world.

As long as there has been hockey, there have been hockey fans. As a fan of the game myself, I've always tried to absorb every little bit of information I could about the game that I grew up playing and the players that I idolized. Each new piece of information that I learned from the back of a hockey card or found in a book made me feel that much closer to the players, and in a competitive way, made me feel like a bigger fan than my friends. Today that greedy need for information has finally paid off.

Canadian Hockey Trivia details some of the most important, least known and just plain strange facts about hockey. However, unlike most other trivia books, I have included more detail beyond the simple facts in order to show a better picture of the most interesting parts of the game. For example, many people know that Darryl Sittler scored the most points in a single NHL game, but they don't know that the goaltender he scored them against, Dave Reece, was nicknamed "In the Wrong Place at the Wrong Time Reece." Most fans also don't know that Joe Malone of the 1920 Québec Bulldogs holds the NHL record for most goals in an NHL game at 7, but Frank McGee of the 1905 Ottawa Silver Seven scored 14 goals in one Stanley Cup game, completely destroying Malone's incredible record.

It's always fun to be able to recite a fact about the game that no one knows, but my favorites have always been the odd stories about the game. Bobby Hull was given the nickname the "Golden Jet" because of his speed on the ice and his gleaming blond mane, but when the Golden One started losing his hair, he switched to a toupee in order to maintain his youthful image. Everyone knew that Hull wore a hairpiece, but no one ever made anything of it because he was a superstar—that is until one game, during a scuffle, when a player named Steve Durbano removed the toupee for all to see.

Another strange story that baffles me to this day happened in 1933 during a Stanley Cup semifinal between the Boston Bruins and the Toronto Maple Leafs. At the end of regulation time, the two teams had yet to score a goal, and after three periods of overtime, the Leafs and Bruins were still tied. With no end in sight, the two teams decided that the only way to end the game would be to flip a coin to see who would move on to the Stanley Cup finals. When the fans got wind of the plan, they booed so loudly that the teams were forced to concede to the crowd's demands and play on. Luckily, the game only lasted a few more minutes until Toronto Maple Leaf Ken Doraty scored in the sixth overtime period to end the second-longest game ever played in NHL history.

Often left out of the trivia books are the contributions that women have made to the sport. While they have been few in number, women's impact on hockey can still be felt today. Lady Byng, wife of Canada's governor general and a lover of the finer points of the game, had a trophy commissioned to be awarded to the player who best displayed sportsmanship and gentlemanly conduct combined with a high level of ability on the ice. Professional hockey has long been the domain of men, but long before Manon Rheaume played in goal for the Tampa Bay Lighting, another woman literally made her mark on hockey when her named was engraved on the Stanley Cup after the Detroit Red Wings, the team she and her family owned, won the Stanley Cup in 1952. Today, women continue to open up the game to a whole new audience that has never before considered taking up the sport once dominated by men.

From the most points scored in a career to the ever-changing rules of the game, *Canadian Hockey Trivia* looks at all aspects of hockey, from the greatest players on the ice to the not-so-famous people who put their mark on the game in some unique ways.

Chapter One

NEED-TO-KNOW TRIVIA

And Hockey Was Born

The battle over where the first hockey game was played continues to this day, with cities all over the world claiming to be the birthplace of the sport. From small towns in the United States to the frozen ponds of Montréal and Halifax, there are many claims to where hockey was born, but the first officially recognized game took place in Montréal on March 3, 1875.

The first "official" game took place at the Victoria Covered Rink at the intersection of Stanley and Drummond in downtown Montréal. Although the rink was mainly used for leisure skating, the rink's surface dimensions (202 feet by 85 feet) provided the standard for what eventually became the modern hockey rink. Several McGill University students played the first game with nine players to each side. A goal was scored when the puck was hit between two posts that were placed 8 feet apart, and defending the goal was not allowed. The game was noted for its quick and rough play. The match ended with one team scoring two "games"—the term "goals" hadn't yet been used—against one "game" for the other team. As reported in the *Montréal Gazette*, turnout was large, and many left the rink that night "quite satisfied with the thrilling evening spectacle."

Penalty Box

Violence in hockey has received a lot of media attention recently, but it has always been part of the game. That night of the first official game, several ladies had to be removed from the arena after fainting because of the violence on the ice.

The First League

In the late 1800s, hockey's popularity was on the rise. Some of the first games played between teams from Montréal and Québec City were so well attended that teams from the two cities decided to form a league. The first organized hockey league, the Amateur Hockey Association of Canada (AHAC), was formed in 1887. There were six participating teams in the AHAC. Four of the teams were from Montréal—Montréal Amateur Athletic Association, Victorias, McGill, and the Crystals. One team was from Ottawa and one from Québec City. The season ran throughout the winter months, and the club at the top of the standings at the end of the regular season could challenge any other team in what was called a challenge series. Until 1893, winners of the challenge series were simply declared champions, but in 1893, Canada's acting governor general, Lord Stanley, purchased a trophy and named it the Dominion Hockey Challenge Cup, to be awarded to the best team in Canada. The first-ever winner of the Dominion Cup (later to be known as the Stanley Cup) was the Montréal Amateur Athletic Association.

Penalty Box

Only amateur teams competed for the Cup until 1910, when the first Canadian professional league, the National Hockey Association (NHA), was formed. The NHA eventually folded, giving way to today's National Hockey League (NHL).

Hockey's First Goal-Scoring Star

Hockey came naturally to Joe Malone. Known for his speed and ability to maneuver around opponents without losing the puck, he quickly earned the nickname "Phantom" because no one on the ice could seem to touch him.

Malone started his professional career with the Québec Bulldogs of the National Hockey Association(NHA) where he played for seven successful years, winning the Stanley Cup twice and recording one of the greatest records in hockey history. On March 8, 1913, during a challenge cup game against Sydney, Nova Scotia, Malone scored 9 goals in a single game, leading his team to their second Stanley Cup victory in a row. Malone's scoring talents continued to shine when he joined the Montréal Canadiens in the newly formed National Hockey League. In just 20 games, he scored an amazing 44 goals, which averages out to an incredible 2.2 goals per game—a record not even Wayne Gretzky came close to beating when he scored his equally incredible 50 goals in 39 games.

Malone added another amazing record to his resume after he had returned to Québec City to play for the Bulldogs during the 1919–20 season. During the final game of the season, Malone scored an NHL-record 7 goals, a feat never since equalled.

Penalty Box

Over his entire career, Malone scored 344 goals in 274 regular season games between 1909 and 1924. This averages out to an incredible 1.3 goals per game. Wayne Gretzky's record 894 goals in 1487 games only averages out to 0.6 goals per game. If Malone had played the same number of games as Gretzky and continued to score at the same rate, he would have scored about 1784 goals!

Lord Stanley's Cup Goes South of the Border

Canadians have always been known as the creators of—and therefore the best at—the game of hockey. But many years ago, when the Stanley Cup measured only a few inches tall, an American team took home the title of the best hockey team in North America. The team to own this distinction was the 1917 Seattle Metropolitans of the Pacific Coast Hockey Association (PCHA).

Back when the Stanley Cup was still a challenge cup, the top teams from the rival NHA and the PCHA competed for the right to be named as Cup champions and the best in the country. At the end of the 1917 season, the Montréal Canadiens won the NHA finals and the right to face off against the PCHA champion Seattle Metropolitans. The Montréal Canadiens travelled to Seattle to play for the Cup. Games one and three were played under PCHA rules (seven players per side, forward passing in the neutral zone allowed and no substitution for penalized players), and games two and four were played under NHA rules (six players per side, no forward passing and substitutions allowed).

The Canadiens, backstopped by goaltending legend George Vezina, won the first game 8–4 but lost the next three games outscored by a margin of 14–3. Metropolitans goaltender Harry "Hap" Holmes was solid in nets, leading his team to their first Stanley Cup victory.

Penalty Box

Although the Metropolitans were the first U.S.-based team to win the Stanley Cup, most of the players on the winning team were actually Canadian.

Willie O'Ree Breaks the Barrier

Although he only lasted 45 games in the National Hockey League (NHL), Willie O'Ree's impact on the sport will last forever.

Throughout the entire history of the NHL, there had not been a single black player to play in a game. That changed when a young player named Willie O'Ree was called up from the minors to play in his first NHL game on January 18, 1958, with the Boston Bruins. Unfortunately, it was the colour of his skin that most people were looking at and not the quality of his game. Head coach Milt Schmidt had a simple answer to all the people that looked at him as anything other than an equal player, "He isn't black, he's a Bruin."

After two games with the Bruins during the 1957–58 season, O'Ree was sent back to the minors. The Bruins called O'Ree back for duty two years later during the 1960–61 season. This time, he remained with the team for 43 games. Despite all the racial slurs and obstacles set before him, O'Ree managed to open the door for players of all different backgrounds.

Penalty Box

Before O'Ree broke the colour barrier in 1957, 10 years earlier another black player was making waves in the minors. In 1947, Herb Carnegie was considered by many to be one of the premier talents in minor hockey, but the colour of his skin kept him from the major leagues.

Just a Few of Gretzky's 61 Records

Most career goals, assists and points: It will likely be many more years before another player comes along to challenge the amazing career-points plateau established by Gretzky. His 894 goals, 1963 assists and 2857 points in 1487 games are a testament to his skill and ability to consistently play at the top of his game.

Most goals in a season: In 1981–82, a young Gretzky scored an incredible 92 goals, completely smashing Phil Esposito's single-season mark of 76 goals in the 1970–71 season with the Bruins. That year, Gretzky also became the first person to break the 200-point mark in NHL history.

Most 40-, 50- and 60-plus–goal seasons: All great players have one thing in common. Consistency. A player can have two amazing years, but he will never be remembered as one of the best if he cannot produce on a regular basis. Gretzky takes the ultimate prize in this category, with 12 40-plus–goal seasons (consecutively), nine 50-plus–goal seasons and five 60-plus–goal seasons. He also managed to sneak in 15 100-plus–point seasons in his career.

Most career playoff goals, assists and points: Over a 20-year period, Gretzky appeared in 208 playoff games and tallied an impressive stats sheet that leaves ample space between himself and all those who come after him. He has scored 122 play-off goals and an incredible 260 assists for a total of 382 points. One-time teammate and friend Mark Messier falls into second place in each category with 109 goals, 186 assists and 295 points in the playoffs.

Most consecutive games points-scoring streak: From the start of the 1983–84 NHL season, Wayne Gretzky managed to score a point in 51 consecutive games. In second place is Mario Lemieux of the 1989–90 Pittsburgh Penguins, with 46 consecutive games.

Most career goals in the all-star game: Being Wayne Gretzky, he got to make a lot of trips to the annual all-star game, and he added another record to his tally by scoring 13 career all-star goals.

Most game-winning goals in the playoffs: Among his 122 playoff goals, Wayne Gretzky was bound to score a few game winners along the way. In his career, he managed to help his team by scoring the winning tally 24 times. That translates to 24 wins he helped secure in the playoffs. No wonder he was a two-time Conn Smythe Trophy winner.

Youngest player to score 50 goals: Although Jimmy Carson of the 1988 Los Angeles Kings also reached the plateau at 19 years of age, Gretzky takes home the record because he was six months younger than Carson was when he achieved the feat.

Gretzky Doesn't Own All the Records

Although the Great One owns and shares 61 records for some the most important milestones in hockey, there remain a considerable number of other players throughout hockey history whose feats managed to escape Gretzky's abilities.

Most games played: "Mr. Hockey" Gordie Howe is likely to hold on to this record for quite some time. Howe played 1767 games in the NHL over six decades. Mark Messier holds second place with 1756 games played.

Most penalty minutes: Not a list Gretzky even registers on, but Dave "Tiger" Williams is still proud of his 3966 penalty minutes served. The only active player who could challenge for most-penalized player is Tie Domi of the Toronto Maple Leafs, with a total of 3443 minutes of time served.

Most goals by a rookie: In the 1992–93 season, rookie sensation Teemu Selanne (nicknamed the "Finnish Flash") scored 76 goals, becoming the first European player to own one of the NHL's major records.

Most Stanley Cup titles: From 1955 to 1975, Henri Richard of the Montréal Canadiens took home 11 Stanley Cup titles. Maurice Richard's younger brother joined the Canadiens at the right time in their history, when they dominated the late '50s, '60s and '70s. Tied for second place are Jean Beliveau and Yvan Cournoyer, with 10 Stanley Cups to their names.

Most penalty minutes in a single season: Dave Schultz's 472 minutes in penalties during the 1974–75 season with the Philadelphia Flyers was one of the major contributing factors to the team's nickname, "The Broad Street Bullies." Since then, only Mike Peluso of the 1991–92 Chicago Blackhawks has come close, with 408 penalty minutes. With the role of the enforcer changing in the more open rules of today's game, it's likely that Schultz's record will stand a long time.

Most points by a defenceman in a single season: Bobby Orr scored 37 goals and 102 assists for 139 points, the most ever by a defenceman in the NHL. Paul Coffey of the 1985–86 Edmonton Oilers came really close when he got 138 points. Since Coffey, there has not been a defenceman who has come anywhere near breaking Orr's record, and one is not likely to come along for a long time, if ever.

Most consecutive years in the playoffs by a player: Larry Robinson owns the distinction of being the only player to appear in 20 consecutive playoff years. His record was set as a member of the Montréal Canadiens and the Los Angeles Kings. Robinson started his playoff run in 1973 and ended it in 1992.

Most goals in one playoff year: Reggie Leach and Jari Kurri share the record, each scoring 19 goals in a single playoff season. Kurri won the Stanley Cup in his record-setting year, but Leach, unfortunately, scored all those goals in vain. Despite his efforts, his Philadelphia Flyers lost to the Montréal Canadiens in the final series.

Most career power-play goals: Left winger Dave Andreychuk broke Phil Esposito's record of 249 power-play goals when he scored his 250th on November 12, 2002. Andreychuk continues to add to his total with the Tampa Bay Lightning.

Most goals in a single NHL game: Although some have come close, no one has yet equalled Joe Malone's amazing record of 7 goals in an NHL game. Playing with the Québec Bulldogs at the time, Joe Malone put his name in the history books on January 31, 1920, when his team went up against the Toronto St. Patricks. Before a sparse crowd of only 1200 people, Joe Malone almost single-handedly beat Toronto by a final score of 10–6. When he was a member of the defunct NHA, he scored 9 goals in one playoff game. Scoring came easily to Malone, so 7 goals really did not seem like much of an accomplishment.

Most goals in a Stanley Cup game: As amazing as Joe Malone's 7 goals and 9 goals in one game were, the most amazing record comes off the golden stick of Frank McGee of the 1905 Ottawa Silver Seven, who scored an incredible 14 goals in one Stanley Cup game against the Dawson City Nuggets.

Fewest goals in a career over 1000 games: Brad Marsh holds the dubious distinction of only scoring 23 goals in a career that lasted 1086 games. That's only 1 goal every 47.2 games, making every goal a cherished event.

Youngest player to lead or share the most-goals title during a regular season: While some might immediately scream out Wayne Gretzky, it was 18-year-old Rick Nash who scored 41 goals, along with Jerome Iginla and Ilya Kovalchuk, to become the youngest player ever to lead the league in goals.

Youngest player to score more than 100 points: Although Gretzky is also a good candidate for this one, he just doesn't compare to the young Dale Hawerchuk's 103 points in 1982 at the age of 18 years, 11 months. Gretzky makes it into second spot at 19 years, 2 months.

The highest-paid player: There is no arguing that Jaromir Jagr is one of the best players in the NHL today and that he is worth every penny to any team that signs him. That's why he fetched

an incredible $88 million for an eight-year con-
tract with the Washington Capitals in 2001. That
would pay him $11 million per year, $134,000
per game, and nearly $45,000 per period. Not bad
for a day's work!

Chapter Two
CANADIAN TEAMS PAST AND PRESENT

Current Teams

Montréal Canadiens

J. Ambrose O'Brien founded the Montréal Canadiens Hockey Club on December 4, 1909. Since that day, the team has been the most dominant force in hockey history, winning 24 Stanley Cups, and has produced some of the best players to step onto the ice. A look at the list of stars that have worn the CH for Montréal over the years is like a trip through the Hockey Hall of Fame.

Over almost a century, the Canadiens have been made up of Hall of Fame members such as Jacques Plante, Howie Morenz, Aurel Joliat, Maurice Richard, Jean Beliveau, Guy Lafleur, Larry Robinson and many others.

But as the years have passed, the Montréal Canadiens have struggled, trying to revive the glories of the past. But with a new lineup of fresh faces, the Canadiens are hoping to rekindle the days of old and take the team to their 25th Stanley Cup championship.

Important Dates

1917—The franchise joins the newly founded National Hockey League, changes its name to the Club de hockey Canadien and develops the famous CH logo on its jerseys.

1919—The last game of the Stanley Cup finals between Montréal and the Seattle Metropolitans is cancelled because of the influenza epidemic.

1924—The Montréal Forum is built.

1937—Howie Morenz dies from injuries sustained during a game.

1955—The Richard Riots shock the hockey world and the country.

1957—The Molson family purchases the Club de hockey Canadien from the Canadian Arena Company.

1960—The Canadiens win their record fifth-straight Stanley Cup.

1993—The Canadiens win their 24th Stanley Cup in a series against the Los Angeles Kings.

1996—The historic Montréal Forum is closed, and the Canadiens move into the Molson Centre (later renamed the Bell Centre).

Ottawa Senators

The Ottawa Senators history must be broken down into two parts. There are the Senators that won four Stanley Cups and were one of the premier teams in the early NHL. Then there are the Senators that rejoined the league in 1992 and missed the play-offs four years in a row but have recently rebounded to their early NHL form to become one of the best offensive teams in the league.

With talents such as Dany Heatley, Daniel Alfredsson, Jason Spezza and Martin Havlat, the new Ottawa Senators are looking more and more like the powerhouse offence of the 1980s Edmonton Oilers.

Important Dates

1920—The Senators win their first NHL Stanley Cup Championship.

1922—The Senators and the Toronto St. Patricks play in the first-ever tie game.

1924—Ottawa's Frank Nighbor wins the first Hart Trophy for the league's most valuable player.

1927—Ottawa wins its fourth and final Stanley Cup championship.

1934—The Ottawa Senators franchise folds, is moved to St. Louis and becomes the St. Louis Eagles.

1992—The Ottawa Senators franchise returns to the NHL.

1996—Ottawa makes the playoffs for the first time in 66 years.

Toronto Maple Leafs

Excluding the Montréal Canadiens, no other team in hockey has such a deep and passionate history as the Toronto Maple Leafs. Although they weren't called the Maple Leafs until 1926, the franchise was at the centre of hockey long before the NHL was born. Toronto won its first Stanley Cup when the team was known as the Blueshirts in 1914. When Toronto joined the new National Hockey League in 1917 as the Toronto Arenas, it was the first team in the league to win the coveted Stanley Cup. Throughout its entire history, the team has won 14 Stanley Cups and has had some of the best players in the annals of hockey to pass through team ranks.

From the start, Toronto had great players such as goaltender Harry Holmes, forward Irvine 'Ace' Bailey, Babe Dye, the great man-behind-the-scenes Conn Smythe, the always-expressive King Clancy, Ted Kennedy, Bill Barilko (famous for scoring the winning goal in overtime to beat the Montréal Canadiens and also for disappearing in a plane crash), Punch Imlach, Turk Broda and many more.

Although the Leafs haven't won the Stanley Cup since 1967, Toronto's fans continue to believe in the team that they have grown up watching for generations.

Important Dates

1917—Toronto wins the NHL's first Stanley Cup as the Toronto Arenas.

1919—The Toronto Arenas change their name to the St. Patricks.

1926—Conn Smythe takes control of the team and renames it the Maple Leafs.

1931—Maple Leaf Gardens opens for business.

1936—Toronto plays the New York Americans in the first game broadcast from coast to coast on Canadian radio.

1951—Bill Barilko disappears in a plane crash up north, and his body is found 10 years later.

1955—The Zamboni makes its first appearance in the NHL in a Canadiens game at Maple Leaf Gardens, on March 10.

1967—The Leafs win the Stanley Cup for the last time.

1999—Maple Leaf Gardens closes, and the team moves to the new Air Canada Centre.

Calgary Flames

When the Atlanta Flames franchise failed and became the Calgary Flames in 1980, hockey quickly established itself as the main sport in town. Calgary fans now had an answer to the freshman Edmonton Oilers team. The Flames started a new life in Calgary at the 6500-seat Stampede Corral with a 5–5 tie against the Québec Nordiques. The Flames even made the playoffs that first year, getting all the way to the semifinals before losing to Minnesota. The team really came into its own when players such as Lanny MacDonald, Al MacInnis, Joe Nieuwendyk and goaltender Mike Vernon joined the team.

These talented players took the Flames all the way to the finals in 1986 and 1989. They lost in their first appearance in the Stanley Cup finals to the Montréal Canadiens but got revenge in 1989, when they beat the Canadiens to take their first-ever Cup.

Unfortunately the Cup and the playoffs seemed to pass Calgary by for the next few years. The team just barely made the playoffs in the early '90s and missed out on them completely for eight years in a row. Things finally changed in 2004, when a young Canadian-born player by the name of Jerome Iginla and a goaltender named Miikka Kiprusoff led their team through one of the most exciting playoff sprints to the Stanley Cup finals, only to lose in game seven against the Tampa Bay Lightning.

Important Dates

1972—The Flames franchise is born—but in Atlanta.

1980—The Atlanta Flames become the Calgary Flames after the team struggles because of financial difficulties.

1981—Hockey's most famous moustached man, Lanny MacDonald, joins the Flames organization.

1983—The Saddledome opens.

1986—The Flames lose in the Stanley Cup finals against the Montréal Canadiens and a rookie goaltender named Patrick Roy.

1989—The Flames have their revenge as they take home the Stanley Cup, beating the Canadiens in six games.

1989—Lanny MacDonald retires from the game.

1996—Jerome Iginla joins the Flames.

2004—After an exciting run to the finals, the Flames lose in a game-seven heartbreaker to the Tampa Bay Lightning.

Vancouver Canucks

Professional hockey had not been played in Vancouver since the 1920s, when the Vancouver Millionaires tore up the Pacific Coast Hockey Association. The city welcomed pro hockey back in 1970 with the arrival of the Vancouver Canucks.

The team first made it into the playoffs in 1975 but didn't really challenge for the Cup until 1994

when they lost a heartbreaker to the New York
Rangers in seven games after an entertaining and
competitive series.

Since then, the Canucks have struggled to make
the playoffs for several seasons, only to recently
bounce back with players such as Trevor Linden,
the Sedin twins, Todd Bertuzzi, Markus Naslund
and goaltender Dan Cloutier.

Important Dates

1970—The Canucks enter the National Hockey
League.

1970—Orland Kurtenbach is named the team's
first captain.

1982—The Canucks lose to the New York Islanders in the Stanley Cup finals.

1991—Pavel Bure plays in his first season.

1994—In their second trip to the Stanley Cup
finals, the Canucks lose in seven games to
the New York Rangers.

2000—Boston Bruin Marty McSorley hits Canucks
player Donald Brashear in the head with
his stick, sending Brashear to the ice in
convulsions. McSorley is found guilty of
assault in criminal court.

2004—Todd Bertuzzi assaults Colorado Avalanche
player Steve Moore with a punch from
behind, knocking Moore unconscious and

sending him to the hospital with a broken neck, concussion and facial lacerations. Bertuzzi is suspended and fined by the league and is charged with assault by a Vancouver criminal court.

Edmonton Oilers

The Edmonton Oilers first came onto the scene for the inaugural season of the World Hockey Association(WHA) in 1972 as the Alberta Oilers. The team spent its first season alternating home games between Calgary and Edmonton, but the idea was abandoned for the start of the 1973 season, and the team's name was changed to the Edmonton Oilers. During the final season of the WHA, Oilers owner Peter Pocklington signed a young phenom by the name of Wayne Gretzky to a 21-year personal-services contract worth $4–5 million. Upon entry into the NHL in 1979, the Oilers used their draft priority to secure Gretzky and select a young teenager named Mark Messier to add more youth to the new franchise.

Along with other stars, including Kevin Lowe, Paul Coffey, Glen Anderson, Esa Tikkanen and Grant Fuhr, coach and general manager Glen Sather moulded his young players into the greatest offensive team in the history of the game.

The Oilers won their first of five Stanley Cups in 1984, defeating the defending champion New York Islanders in five games. In the past few years, they have had a talented pool of young players pass through their ranks, but they could never seem to find their winning ways, despite great players such as Doug Weight, Bill Guerin, Curtis Joseph, Eric Brewer and fan favourite Ryan Smyth.

Giving up players such as Eric Brewer, Jeff Woywitka and Doug Lynch wasn't easy for Edmonton Oilers general manager Kevin Lowe, but when you are able to sign veteran defence-man Chris Pronger to a five-year, $31.25 million contract, a few sacrifices have to be made. Pronger did not disappoint the Oilers' faithful, as he was one of the major ingredients in the Oilers' incred-ible run to the Stanley Cup finals against the Carolina Hurricanes in 2006. The Oilers came back from the series 3–1 deficit but unfortunately they lost in game seven by a score of 3–1. So it came as a big shock to the media and to Edmon-ton fans when Pronger requested a trade imme-diately after the finals. The official explanation for the trade was for personal reasons; however, many theories abound as to the actual reason Pronger wanted out of Edmonton. On July 3, 2006, Pronger was traded to Anaheim for Joffrey Lupul, Ladislav Smid and draft picks in 2007 and 2008.

Important Dates

1972—The franchise starts out as the Alberta Oilers, part of the new professional league, the World Hockey Association.

1979—The Edmonton Oilers of the WHA sign 18-year-old Wayne Gretzky to a multi-year agreement.

1979—Edmonton wins an NHL franchise and plays its first game before a sell-out crowd.

1979—Rookie Wayne Gretzky ties Marcel Dionne in scoring, finishing the season with 137 points.

1982—Gretzky finishes the season with a record-setting 92 goals.

1984—The Edmonton Oilers win their first Stanley Cup.

1984—The Edmonton Oilers beat the Minnesota North Stars 12–8, setting a modern-day NHL record for the most goals by two teams in a game.

1986—Coffey breaks Bobby Orr's goals-scoring record of 46 goals, scoring 48 of his own.

1988—In the most famous trade in hockey history, Wayne Gretzky is traded to the Los Angeles Kings.

1990—Led by Mark Messier, the Oilers win a fifth Stanley Cup.

1993—The Oilers miss the playoffs for the first time in their history.

2006—Oilers just miss a sixth Stanley Cup in a heart-breaking game seven against the Carolina Hurricanes.

Teams from Another Era

Winnipeg Jets

The World Hockey Association version of the Winnipeg Jets enjoyed seven successful years in the league, winning the Avco Cup three times. When the league ran into financial troubles in the late '70s, only four teams survived the switchover to the NHL, including the Jets.

The WHA team the people of Winnipeg had grown to love was forced to release all its players except two skaters and two goalies in the 1979 expansion draft. The new Winnipeg Jets had a difficult time in their first two years in the NHL, but this allowed them top pick in the 1981 draft, and they selected Cornwall Royals sensation Dale Hawerchuk. The team's fortunes quickly turned around with the new talent on the roster, but they were stuck in the same division as the high-scoring Edmonton Oilers of the '80s. The Jets could never make it out of the division round in the playoffs.

Even the introduction of rookie sensation Teemu Selanne in 1992 could not lift the Jets to new heights. Then along came the lockout-shortened season, which started the process in motion for the Jets' eventual move to Phoenix. The team could no longer sustain the rising salaries and the demand to build a new stadium. After the 1996 season, the Jets were forced to sell the franchise when bids to save the team failed. Today, the Jets are known as the Phoenix Coyotes.

Important Dates

1972—The Winnipeg Jets play their first game in the professional World Hockey Association.

1979—After the WHA is dismantled, the Winnipeg Jets join the National Hockey League.

1981—After a 9–57–14 record, the Jets get first pick overall in the draft and select Dale Hawerchuk.

1988—The Jets lose again in the playoffs to the Edmonton Oilers in five games. Their record against the Oilers in the playoffs stands at one win and 18 losses.

1990—Dale Hawerchuk is traded to the Buffalo Sabres.

1993—Teemu Selanne scores 76 goals in his rookie season and takes home the Calder Trophy, beating out Eric Lindros and Felix Potvin.

1996—The Jets lose to the Detroit Red Wings in the first round of the playoffs, ending nearly three decades of professional hockey in the city of Winnipeg.

1997—The team becomes the Phoenix Coyotes.

Québec Nordiques

The Québec Nordiques joined the World Hockey Association in its inaugural season in 1972 and were immediately compared with their provincial counterparts in the National Hockey League, the Montréal Canadiens. They won the WHA's Avco Cup in 1974, but the team's exploits could not hold the attention of the province when the Montréal Canadiens dominated the NHL. So when the Québec Nordiques joined the NHL in 1979, an instant rivalry was born.

Headed by coach Jacques Demers, the Nordiques entered the league with a talented pool of players such as Real Cloutier and Robbie Ftorek, and they picked up Michel Goulet, Dale Hunter, and most significantly, Anton Stastny in their inaugural draft. Anton was later joined by his brother Peter, and the brothers became one of the most effective duos for the club. The "Battle of Québec" was set to heat up nicely. Both teams were in the same division and had played each other several times during the season, making for a bitter rivalry as they battled for playoff positions.

Québec had its last appearance against the Canadiens in the 1993 playoffs, with players including Valeri Kamensky, Adam Foote, Joe Sakic and Owen Nolan. They lost the series but returned over the next two years with amazing regular season results and a host of young players ready to build for the future.

Then the really bad news hit the team. Financial troubles plagued the Nordiques, despite having one of the most talented teams on paper, and management could not convince enough investors or the government to help prop them up. Les Nordiques played their last game against the Rangers on May 16 and announced on July 1, 1995, that the franchise was moving to Colorado.

Important Dates

1972—The Nordiques join the World Hockey Association.

1979—After the WHA disbands, the Nordiques are awarded an NHL franchise.

1982—The team eliminates the Montréal Canadiens for the first time in the first round of the playoffs. The Battle of Québec is established.

1985—The Nordiques and the Canadiens brawl in one of the most violent and penalized games in the playoffs.

1987—Joe Sakic is drafted.

1993—The Nordiques are eliminated once again by the eventual Stanley Cup champions, the Montréal Canadiens.

1995—The franchise moves to Colorado and becomes the Avalanche. They win the Stanley Cup the next season, leaving a bitter taste in Nordiques fans' mouths.

Québec Bulldogs

The formation of the Québec Bulldogs can be traced back to the formation of the first Amateur Hockey Association of Canada in 1886. When the first professional league was formed, the National Hockey Association, the Québec Bulldogs were left out but were finally accepted into the fold in 1909. The team went on to win two Stanley Cups in 1912 and 1913, with future Hall of Fame players such as Joe Malone, Paddy Moran, Joe Hall and Russell Crawford. Although the team was based in the capital, only a few players in the team's history were French. Even the name Bulldogs was chosen as a reminder of the team's link to Britain.

When the Bulldogs eventually joined the NHL in 1919 after recalling many of its players from the original team, including Malone and Hall, the team just weren't the same. The only highlights the team had that season came from Malone, who led the league in scoring and scored a record 7 goals in one game on January 31, 1920, against the Toronto St. Patricks. After just four wins and

20 losses during the season, the team packed up and left town to become the Hamilton Tigers. Québec City would have to wait for the arrival of the Nordiques in 1979 to see another NHL game.

Important Dates

1909—The Bulldogs officially join the National Hockey Association.

1912—The team wins its first Stanley Cup.

1913—The Bulldogs win a second consecutive Cup.

1917—The financially troubled Bulldogs fail to become a member of the new National Hockey League.

1919—The team joins the NHL for one year before moving to Hamilton.

1920—Joe Malone scores an NHL-record 7 goals in one game.

Hamilton Tigers

The Abso-Pure Ice Company had just built a 4000-seat artificial rink in Hamilton and was looking for a team to fill the stands when the Québec Bulldogs franchise was in financial trouble. The company's timing was perfect. Abso-Pure paid $5000 for the franchise and started operations the following season. But the losing ways of the franchise continued, even with the addition of Babe Dye, Joe Matte and

Joe Malone, winning just six games in their first season.

Even with the legendary Art Ross jumping on board as coach for the 1922–23 season, the Tigers still could not win more than six games. Yet Hamilton was not defeated. With the signing of brothers Red and Shorty Green, and Alex McKinnon and Charlie Langlois, the team's fortunes began to turn around. They finished the season at the top of the league with a 19–10–1 record and were waiting for the winner of the Montréal Canadiens and Toronto St. Patricks series to decide the NHL champion. But on March 9,1925, before playing a single playoff game, 10 players got together and demanded that they receive an extra $200 for the upcoming games. The players felt that their contracts were only valid for regular season play and that all the other teams were giving their players bonuses for the playoffs. But Hamilton management held firm and refused to give in to the players' demands. The league promptly suspended the team and handed the NHL championship to the Montréal Canadiens. The Tigers were sold the next season to New York for $75,000, and the franchise became known as the New York Americans.

Important Dates

1920—The Québec Bulldogs franchise is sold to the Hamilton Abso-Pure Ice Company and changes its name to the Hamilton Tigers.

1920—The Tigers play the first of four straight losing seasons.

1925—The team finishes the season in first place but is suspended after contract negotiations go bad, and the franchise is eventually sold to New York.

Montréal Maroons

For 14 seasons in the NHL, Montréal was home to two teams: the Maroons and the Canadiens.

In their first season, the Montréal Maroons had mainly veteran players living out the final years of their professional hockey days, and the age showed on the ice as they missed the playoffs that first season. The addition of great players like Nels Stewart and goaltender Clint Benedict helped the Maroons climb back into contention in the league. Veteran talent won them their first Cup against the Victoria Cougars in 1926, the final year that the Cup was given out as a challenge cup.

The Maroons went on to win another Stanley Cup in 1935, but when they failed to make the playoffs in 1938, and with the threat of World War II making the economic viability of the team uncertain, the owners asked the league if operations could be suspended for a year. The NHL granted this request, but the Maroons never returned to the league. The franchise was dismantled, leaving the Canadiens as the sole Montréal team in the NHL.

Important Dates

1924—After a group of business partners get together and build the Montréal Forum, the Montréal Professional Hockey Club is formed to occupy the building.

1925—The Montréal Professional Hockey Club changes its name to the Montréal Maroons, named after the colour of their uniforms.

1926—With Clint Benedict, Nels Stewart and Babe Siebert, the Montréal Maroons take home a first Stanley Cup championship, beating the Victoria Cougars in four games.

1935—The Maroons win a second Stanley Cup championship.

1938—The Maroons suspend operations because of financial uncertainty prior to World War II.

1939—The Maroons owners advise the NHL that they will no longer be operating a franchise.

Montréal Wanderers

Although they only played six games in the NHL, the Montréal Wanderers remain one of the most legendary teams in hockey history, responsible for producing some of the most notable names to play the game. Hall of Fame stars like Lester Patrick, Art Ross and Ernie Russell all played for the team before they joined the NHL.

When the new National Hockey League was formed, the Wanderers were included for the start of the new season. With World War I depleting many of the quality players, the Wanderers were forced to start the season with a team of aging veterans. Owner Sam Lichtenhein threatened to withdraw from the league if he could not get a fresh supply of young players from the other teams after a series of embarrassing losses. The league and the other owners refused, and when a fire destroyed the Montréal Arena, the team withdrew its franchise from the National Hockey League.

Important Dates

1903—The Montréal Wanderers join the Federal Amateur Hockey League.

1906—Now part of the Eastern Canada Amateur Hockey Association, the Wanderers defeat the Ottawa Silver Seven on a pair of goals by Lester Patrick to win a first Stanley Cup.

1907—The team wins its second Stanley Cup.

1908—The Wanderers win a third Stanley Cup.

1910—They join the new National Hockey Association and win a fourth and final Stanley Cup.

1918—After just six games, two of which the team defaulted, the Wanderers are forced to withdraw from the league after they suffer a terrible season because of a lack of young, quality players and their arena burns down.

Chapter Three

THE MOST AMAZING FEATS ON ICE

AND TONIGHT'S THREE STARS ARE...

In 1944, the Montréal Canadiens took on the Toronto Maple Leafs in game two of the Stanley Cup semifinals. The Leafs held the Canadiens off the score sheet in the first period, thanks to some tight checking on Maurice Richard by Leafs veteran Bob Davidson. Richard was fuming during the first intermission and swore to his teammates that they could turn things around.

A man of his word, Richard did not waste time putting the Canadiens on the board, with a goal just two minutes in and a second goal just 17 seconds later. Moments later, Richard took a pass from Toe Blake and scored his first Stanley Cup hat trick. Before long, Richard found himself in front of the Leafs goaltender again and potted his fourth goal of the game. The fans erupted in applause when Richard scored his fifth and final goal.

After the teams skated off the ice, Richard waited in the dressing room for the stars to be announced, certain that he would be named first star after his performance. Much to the surprise of Richard and the fans, Richard was announced as the third star, setting off a loud chorus of boos and French curses. When Richard was named second star, a few of the fans who could hear the announcement caught on. Slowly, the boos turned to wild cheers when the first star was announced. Hats and programs began to litter the ice as Richard received one of the greatest ovations of his career—the only time in the NHL that a player was awarded all three stars.

Sittler's Shining Night

It started out as just a regular game between the Boston Bruins and the Toronto Maple Leafs, but when it was all said and done, the game held on February 7, 1976, went down in the history books.

Bruins coach Don Cherry, buoyed by his team's recent successes, decided to play rookie Dave Reece in goal instead of his regular solid goaltender Gerry Cheevers. It was a decision that Cherry would ultimately regret.

From the moment the puck was dropped, it was clear that the Maple Leafs, led by captain Darryl Sittler, were in control of the game. The Bruins could hardly get out of their own end, let alone get a play started, while the Leafs tight forechecking and aggressive offence pounded the rookie netminder shot after shot. Sittler finished the game, scoring 10 points on the frazzled Bruins goalie. The total of 6 goals and 4 assists set a league record for points in a single game (previously held by Maurice Richard with 8 points).

"As much as the fans fault Reece for what happened, it was simply a night where every shot and pass I made seemed to pay off in a goal," recalled Sittler. "I hit the corners a couple of times, banking shots in off the post. He didn't really flub one goal."

The Fastest Hat Trick

The 1951–52 season for the Chicago Blackhawks was one of their worst in their history. They had the worst record in the league, and the empty seats at the arena showed that their fans had lost faith that the Hawks could ever come out of their slump. The Blackhawks were clearly not going to make the playoffs that year. The only shining light for the Hawks was a large right-winger named Bill Mosienko.

Despite the odds against him, Mosienko's most memorable moment came at the end of the 1952 regular season. On March 23, 1952, Mosienko secured himself a place in the annals of hockey history.

The game got underway, and the New York Rangers had control of the game from the start. By the end of the second period, the Rangers had amassed a 6–2 lead. Mosienko had different plans and brought his team closer with his first goal at the 6:09 mark of the third period. A few seconds later, he scored his second goal on a surprised Rangers goaltender Lorne Anderson. Mosienko's third goal came at the 6:30 mark after a teammate won the face-off and got the puck to his defence-man, who noticed that Mosienko had gotten behind the defence and fed him a tape-to-tape pass. Lorne Anderson couldn't do anything as Mosienko deked around him and buried the puck in the upper part of the net. Mosienko had scored 3 goals in 21 seconds, a record that still stands to this day. (The only player to come close was Jean Beliveau of the 1955 Montréal Canadiens, who scored 3 power-play goals in 44 seconds.) Inciden-tally, the Blackhawks went on to win the game 7–6 on a pair of late goals scored by Syd Finney.

The Silver Fox Saves the Day

The legendary Lester Patrick was known during his playing days as one of the best forwards of his time, but he will always be remembered for one great game in nets.

During the 1928 Stanley Cup finals between head coach Lester Patrick's New York Rangers and the Montréal Maroons, Rangers goaltender Lorne Chabot was struck in the face with a puck and was taken out of the game. Not wanting to forfeit the game because they didn't have another goaltender, the 44-year-old Patrick decided he would rather take the goalie's place than lose on a technicality.

After taking a few minutes to strap on Chabot's wet pads and do a little stretching, Patrick made his way to the Rangers net. Patrick only let in a single goal and made some good saves as the Rangers put a solid defence in front of their coach and finally won the game in overtime. In the end he made 17 saves on 18 shots. The coach's stint in goal was short-lived. Patrick took his place back behind the bench for the rest of the series and led his team to the Stanley Cup.

Gretzky's 50 Goals in 39 Games

Of all Wayne Gretzky's amazing achievements, the record that is most likely to stand the test of time is his 50 goals in 39 games. Ever since Maurice Richard scored the first 50 goals in 50 games in 1945, hitting the plateau of an average one goal per game has remained one of hockey's most mythical barriers. That is, until Gretzky came along.

Gretzky's shining moment came on December 30, 1981, against the Philadelphia Flyers in the last game before the New Year. The Flyers were a large team that had earned their nickname, the "Broad Street Bullies", and had a tough time defending against the speedier Edmonton Oilers. Gretzky had already potted 4 goals on goaltender Pete Peeters by the third period, but the Flyers were still only a single goal down. Philadelphia pulled their goaltender in a last-ditch effort to tie the game. With under a minute remaining, Gretzky had the puck and a clear path to the net. He took the shot, and it hit the back of the net for his 50th goal. The Oilers bench flooded the ice as the crowd stood to give the visiting player his well-deserved applause.

After the game Gretzky faced a barrage of questions from the media. "Now that you have 50 goals in 39 games, do you think you'll break Esposito's 76 regular season goals? You seem to be on pace to do so," asked one inquisitive reporter.

Gretzky humbly replied, "To hit 76, I'd have to get 26 goals in 40 games. Never mind what's happened up 'til now; that's a lot of goals."

Not only did Gretzky go on to break Esposito's record of 76 goals, but he also finished the season with an amazing 92 goals and 120 assists for a total of 212 points.

Penalty Box

Gretzky was also the first player in NHL history to break the 200-point mark and remains the only one to have done so to this day. Only Mario Lemieux of the 1989 Pittsburgh Penguins came close to the 200-point plateau, missing it by just one point at the end of the regular season.

Chris Nilan Loves Penalties

The honour for the most penalties in one game goes to the Boston Bruins Chris Nilan during a game against the Hartford Whalers on March 31, 1991. It is no surprise that the long-time agitator and confessed tough guy earned the dubious distinction, since he is currently ninth on the all-time penalty minutes list.

That night, it seemed that every time that Nilan stepped onto the ice he was assessed a penalty for an infraction. He was given six minor penalties, two majors, a misconduct and a game misconduct for his behaviour that night. In total, Nilan received a record 10 penalties for a total of 42 minutes in the sin bin.

Would You Like a Little Hockey with Your Fight?

Ask people what team they most expect to be involved in an NHL game with the most penalty minutes handed out, and they would probably answer the Philadelphia Flyers. They would be right. As the history of the Flyers has shown, they have always been a physical team, but no one would have expected the 2004 Ottawa Senators to be their accomplice in the NHL game with the most penalty minutes.

The fight-filled match between the two teams occurred on March 5, 2004. It wasn't just the regular tough guys who got involved in this physical game. Even top scorers like the Flyers' Simon Gagne and the Senators' Daniel Alfredsson were involved in the melees. After the smoke had finally cleared and the teams were sent to their respective dressing rooms, the referees had called 419 minutes in penalties.

Oldest Player in Hockey

The record for the oldest player ever to lace on his skates for a professional hockey team goes to Mr. Hockey himself, Gordie Howe, who at age 52 played a full 80-game season with the Hartford Whalers. Howe scored a respectable 15 goals and had 26 assists.

Hockey's current iron man is Chris Chelios of the Detroit Red Wings, who's still going strong at age 44. He began his career with the Montréal Canadiens in 1983 and hasn't taken a break since. By the way he continues to play, he still has a few years left in him.

Penalty Box

The youngest player ever to play in the NHL was Armand "Bep" Guidolin, who was only 16 years old when he joined the Boston Bruins in November 1942. Most of the older players were off fighting in World War II.

Malik Ends the Longest Shootout

On a Saturday night in New York, the Washington Capitals met the New York Rangers in Madison Square Garden and played a hard-fought, exciting game that ended in a 2–2 tie by the end of the five-minute overtime. Tension in the crowd mounted as goaltenders Olaf Kolzig and Henrik Lundqvist got ready to meet the barrage of players in the shootout.

Both teams matched each other in some beautiful goals and some equally amazing saves, all the way through to the 30th player into the 14th round. After the 29th player had taken his turn, the Rangers head coach had run out of his normal offence-minded players and chose defenceman Marek Malik to take the shot. Malik was a risk, since he had not scored a goal in 21 months, but the coach gave him a try.

Malik did not disappoint. While skating in on Kolzig, Malik passed the puck behind himself and shot it from between his legs over a surprised Kolzig, just under the crossbar, to end the game for the final Rangers 3–2 victory.

Kolzig paid his respects to Malik after the game: "I didn't expect a guy like that to make a move like that. That's something you see in practice. Give the guy credit—he has the [guts] to pull it off."

Alexander Ovechekin Scores on His Back

Sounds impossible, but it's true. The Russian rookie playing for the Washington Capitals is known for his flair and creativity on the ice, but he even surprised himself with this goal. Words can barely do the goal justice—it has to be seen to be believed!

On January 16, 2006, the Washington Capitals had a 5–1 lead over the Phoenix Coyotes when Ovechekin got the puck at centre ice and made his way into the Coyotes' zone. Cutting across the zone, Ovechekin found himself one-on-one with defenceman Paul Mara. Unable to stop Ovechekin, Mara dragged him down onto the ice, hoping to stop him from scoring. Normally, that tactic would work, but not with the most exciting player of the 2005–06 season.

As Ovechekin fell to the ice and slid on his back, he managed to find the puck that was now above his head and took a blind shot that made it past the stunned Phoenix goaltender. Ovechekin himself could hardly believe he had scored the goal, let alone the thousands of spectators who had seen it with their own eyes.

"That was lucky," said Ovechkin. "I saw replay. It was beautiful."

Chapter Four

THE BEST ALWAYS HAPPENS IN THE PLAYOFFS

The Leafs' Incredible Comeback

No one has ever been able to match the Toronto Maple Leafs' comeback Stanley Cup victory of 1942. The Leafs remain the only team in NHL history ever to come back from a 3–0 series deficit in a best of seven Stanley Cup final and win.

The Leafs went into the series against the Detroit Red Wings as the heavy favourites, having finished 15 points ahead during the regular season. However, the Red Wings caught the Leafs by playing a smart, systematic game, and by the third game of the series the Leafs were down 3–0 and faced a long summer ahead. But Leafs coach Hap Day was not yet finished. He had come too far and waited too long for his shot at the Stanley Cup. Day even read a letter to his players from a 14-year-old girl who asked her team to keep fighting and bring home the Cup. The tactics seemed to work, as the Leafs won game four by the slim margin of 4–3. To everyone's surprise, the Leafs won the next two games, tying the series and sending it into the deciding game seven.

The game started off with a pair of goals by both teams, yet the game looked completely in the hands of the Toronto Maple Leafs. Toronto's Pete Langelle scored the winner and Sweeney Schriner scored the insurance goal to give the Leafs a 3–1 victory and take the championship.

Penalty Box

The only other team to come back from a 3–0 deficit in a playoff series was the New York Islanders in the 1975 quarterfinals against the Pittsburgh Penguins. They almost repeated the amazing feat in the next round against the Philadelphia Flyers but could not win in game seven.

Mud's Longest Game

In the first game of the 1936 playoffs the Canadian division champion Montréal Maroons were set to take on their rival American division champs, the Detroit Red Wings, in a best of five series. Only 9000 fans showed up at the Montréal Forum to see the two teams play in what was expected to be an overly defensive game.

The two teams had not put any points on the board by the end of the third period, thanks to some spectacular goaltending from both sides. So into overtime they went. The second overtime passed, then the third, fourth and fifth, until the game reached the sixth overtime period at 2:00 in the morning. The radio announcer began to joke that the Forum staff should be providing beds, but relief came soon.

The only goal of the game came at the 17-minute mark of the sixth overtime period. Detroit forward Hec Kilrea got hold of the puck and charged his way into the Maroons defensive zone, looking to win the game with one shot. As he wound up, Mud Bruneteau positioned himself near the net, hoping for a rebound. Bruneteau got the rebound and poked it past a surprised Chabot into the net. The crowd paused in disbelief, not knowing whether to boo the Red Wings for winning or to cheer Bruneteau for ending the game at 2:25 AM.

In the end, Red Wings goaltender Normie Smith made 90 saves compared to Chabot's 68 in an amazing 176.5 minutes of play. Mud Bruneteau would forever be remembered for scoring the winning goal.

Penalty Box

The second-longest game in NHL history was just three years earlier than Detroit's win in 1936, in a game between the Toronto Maple Leafs and the Boston Bruins that lasted 164.46 minutes. The game was another defensive sleeper with Ken Doraty of the Toronto Maple Leafs scoring the game-winning goal. The third longest was in the 2000 playoffs in a game between the Philadelphia Flyers and the Pittsburgh Penguins. Keith Primeau scored the winner for Philadelphia 152.01 minutes into the game.

Heads or Tails

During the 1933 semifinals between the Boston Bruins and the Toronto Maple Leafs, one of the strangest things in hockey history happened. With the best of five series tied at two games apiece, game five would decide who would move on to the final round to face the New York Rangers for the Stanley Cup. Neither team wanted to give the other any open ground, and they battled to a scoreless tie by the end of regulation time. The problem was that the defensive battle continued into the night, and after several overtime periods the score was still stuck at zero. Both goaltenders refused to give ground, keeping their teams in the game with some spectacular saves. But as the game dragged on into the fifth overtime period with no end in sight, both teams came to the baffling conclusion that the series should be decided with the flip of a coin. Heads, you play for the Stanley Cup; tails, you lose and are soon playing golf.

As soon as the exhausted fans woke up and realized what was about to happen, they began to boo so loudly that the two teams had to abandon their coin-toss plans for fear that a riot would break out. With reluctance, the two exhausted teams skated back out on the ice. The end finally came in the sixth overtime period. Ken Doraty of the Toronto Maple Leafs scored the series winner, to the great relief of everyone in the building that night.

Mr. Sudden Death Mel Hill

Just before World War II, the Boston Bruins played in the opening rounds of the 1939 playoffs against the tough-checking New York Rangers. The Rangers were a defensive team, so they weren't worried about the offensive capabilities of the Bruins Mel Hill (10 regular season goals) going into the third overtime of game one. The Rangers were surprised when Hill took a Bill Cowley pass and scored the winner near the end of the period.

Just two nights later in Boston, the same scenario played out. With the game only in the first overtime period, Cowley again caught Hill with a pass, and Hill made the game-winning goal. No player had ever scored two playoff overtime goals in consecutive games before, and Hill wasn't even finished.

The Rangers battled hard to come back and forced the Bruins into a deciding seventh game. When the game went into the extra periods, all attention turned to Boston's Mel Hill, who had earned the nickname "Sudden Death" for his overtime heroics. Hill secured a place in hockey history when he scored another winner in triple overtime to win the game and the series for the Bruins. Carrying on the momentum from the nail-biter series against the Rangers, the Bruins went on to defeat the Toronto Maple Leafs and won the Stanley Cup.

The Player Who Scored the Game Winner on a Broken Leg

It doesn't sound like it would be possible, but Bob Baun of the 1964 Toronto Maple Leafs actually did score an overtime goal on a broken leg.

The Maple Leafs faced off against the Detroit Red Wings in a bid for their third Cup in a row. With the Wings up in the series 3–2, the Leafs needed hard work and a little luck to win the Cup. With the score tied at 3–3 at about halfway through the third period, Gordie Howe crossed the Leafs blue line and shot at the Leafs net. Unfortunately for defenceman Bob Baun, the frozen puck found its way between his skate boot and the shin guard, sending a sharp pain up Baun's leg.

Baun fell to the ice, clutching his leg in pain. The game was stopped as the medics loaded Baun onto a stretcher. Doctors suspected his leg might be broken, but Baun shrugged off their concerns and returned for the start of the overtime period. After intercepting a Red Wing clearing attempt, Baun crossed into the Detroit zone and fired a shot toward the net that hit one of their defencemen and bounced past the goaltender for the game-winning goal.

Baun was noticeably in pain after the game but refused to see the doctors because he knew that if they found a broken bone he would not be allowed to play in game seven. Despite his obvious injury,

Baun soldiered on and helped the Leafs to their third straight Stanley Cup. After all the celebrations, Baun finally had an x-ray, which confirmed that he had played two games on a broken shinbone.

Demers Makes the Call

In the playoffs, every moment and every little decision counts. For the 1993 Montréal Canadiens, victory and defeat were often too close to call, and every little advantage they had helped them advance through the early rounds. For the Stanley Cup finals against the Los Angeles Kings, the story remained the same. Sometimes to win you needed luck on your side—or a little inside information about the other team.

During the first game of the series, which the Canadiens lost 5–1, a few of the Montréal players noticed that defenceman Marty McSorley's stick blade looked a little odd, curving more to the right than most sticks. The Canadiens players brought this information back to their head coach, Jacques Demers, who decided to hold onto the information until the right time.

That time came in the second game of the series, when the Canadiens were down 2–1 with less than two minutes remaining in the period. Demers asked the referee to check McSorley's stick for an illegal curve, hoping the ace up his sleeve would pay off. Demers' instincts were good, and McSorley was assessed a two-minute penalty that the

Canadiens used to tie the game. The Canadiens went on to win the game and the series to take home their 24th Stanley Cup.

A Strange Victory

Every little boy dreams of growing up to score the game-winning goal in overtime to win the Stanley Cup, but Brett Hull never thought his moment of glory would be tainted by his toe.

The Buffalo Sabres and the Dallas Stars faced off against each other in the 1999 Stanley Cup finals in a defensive series. The Stars had taken the 3–2 series lead going into game six and were looking to end the finals quickly. However, the Sabres were not going down easily and took game six to the last moment before one of the strangest Stanley Cup final endings.

That year, the league had decided to enforce the player in the goaltender's crease rule to the letter. If any part of the player's body found its way into the crease when a goal was scored, it would be immediately disallowed, even if the offending part did not interfere with the goalie.

With the score tied at 1–1, Dallas and Buffalo headed into overtime. But it wasn't until the third overtime that Brett Hull smacked in a rebound in front of Buffalo goaltender Dominic Hasek, ending the game and sending the Dallas bench streaming onto the ice. The problem was that when Hull put the puck into the net, his skate just happened to be a few inches over the crease—clearly visible in the video replay. Buffalo tried to protest and have the goal reviewed, but the celebration had already begun.

Winning One for Ray

After 20 years as a Boston Bruin, Raymond Bourque wanted to win the Stanley Cup. The Hall of Fame defenceman was the centre of the Bruins team, but he wanted a legitimate shot at winning the Stanley Cup one last time before he retired. The Bruins were nowhere near that goal during the 1999–2000 season, sitting at the bottom of the Northeast division. Bourque knew he had only a couple of years left in him and requested he be traded to a contending team. With just 14 games remaining in another possible season without the Cup, Bourque was off to the Colorado Avalanche. The Boston Bruins fans graciously accepted his trade after the 20 loyal years he spent as the heart and soul of the team and the city.

He didn't win the Stanley Cup in 2000 after the Avalanche were eliminated from the playoffs by the Dallas Stars in the conference finals. Bourque extended his career for another season to give it one last chance before finally retiring from the game. By the end of the regular season things were looking bright for Bourque after the Avalanche finished atop the league with 118 points. The team was the odds-on favourite to make it into the finals. The Avalanche beat the Vancouver Canucks, Los Angeles Kings, St. Louis Blues and New Jersey Devils to take home their second Cup in franchise history and the first for Ray Bourque. Captain Joe Sakic accepted the Cup from commissioner Gary Bettman and immediately handed it over to Bourque, who after 21 years in the NHL finally got what he wanted.

Chapter Five

LADIES' NIGHT

The Women Behind the Mask

It was just before the Tampa Bay Lightning's first season in the National Hockey League, and general manager Phil Esposito decided to try something that had never been done in NHL history: let a woman play in an NHL game.

Esposito knew exactly what he was doing when he signed Manon Rheaume to a professional contract in August 1992, and so did everybody in the hockey world. She was athletic, hard working and approachable—and she was attractive. It smelled of a publicity stunt. But the ploy worked like a charm. Rheaume's face was plastered across every newspaper; she was in demand for countless interviews; and the player was on everyone's television set before she even stepped out on the ice.

Rheaume's 15 minutes of NHL fame came in a September 1992 exhibition game against the St. Louis Blues. She stopped the first three shots that came her way but then let one slip by. After shaking off the initial nerves, she only let in one more goal. As the buzzer sounded, the crowd gave Rheaume a warm round of applause. The Québec City native finished the period having let in 2 goals on nine shots. Wendell Young, the next Lightning goaltender in nets, let in 2 goals as well.

Regardless of the Lightning's motives, Manon Rheaume accomplished something that had never been done, and she did not bend before all the media pressure. She never did get the chance to play in a regular season game, but she was signed to a three-year contract with the Lightning's farm team.

Penalty Box

Manon Rheaume wore the number 33 on her jersey for her one game appearance with the Tampa Bay Lightning. Rheaume's favourite goaltender was Patrick Roy, who also wore number 33.

Tough Cookie

Long before her 18th birthday, people had been remarking on how good a hockey player Hayley Wickenheiser was, comparing her style of play to Eric Lindros and—on some occasions—even to the Great One himself. But all the attention and accolades could not turn Wickenheiser's focus from the game she loved. After several years on the

Canadian National Women's team, winning Olympic gold and several World Championship titles, Wickenheiser needed a new challenge. She decided that the only remaining hurdle left in her career as a hockey player was to play in a men's professional league.

Wickenheiser got her chance when she signed a 30-day tryout contract with Kirkkonummi Salamat, a men's team from Finland's second division. Newspapers and media outlets from around the world descended on the small Finnish town not used to such international attention and waited for Wickenheiser to hit the ice in her first game. She played well, not shying away from hits that the other team seemed eager to dish out, and got an assist on a goal. But the media would have to wait until February 1, 2003, for her to become the first woman to score a goal in a men's professional league.

Penalty Box

While she was the first woman to record a goal and assist in a men's professional league, Wickenheiser was not the first woman to play with the big boys. Manon Rheaume played a game with the NHL's Tampa Bay Lightning in 1992, but it was only an exhibition game. Erin Whitten played in nets for the Adirondack Red Wings of the American Hockey League in 1993, becoming the first woman to win a professional men's game on October 30.

Lady Byng

Not just a trophy, Lady Evelyn Byng was the wife of Canada's governor general, Sir Julian Hedworth Georges Byng (1921–26), and a well-known lover of hockey. After attending so many games, Lady Byng developed a liking for the more refined aspects of the game, preferring players who showed proper conduct on the ice combined with skill for the game. In 1925, the Lady Byng Trophy was first awarded to the player who exhibited the best sportsmanship and gentlemanly conduct combined with a high standard of playing ability. Frank Nighbor of the Ottawa Senators was the inaugural winner of the honour. When Lady Byng died in 1949, the trophy was renamed the Lady Byng Memorial Trophy to commemorate her contribution to the game.

Penalty Box

Frank Boucher of the New York Rangers (1926–44) was given the original trophy to keep because he had won it so often—seven times in eight years (1927–35)—that he practically owned it. A new trophy was forged to replace the one given to Boucher.

The First Woman on the Stanley Cup

Marguerite Norris and her family purchased the Detroit Red Wings in 1932. When her father James Norris Sr. passed away in 1952, control of the team passed into her hands. That season also happened to be the year the Red Wings won eight straight playoff games to take home the Stanley Cup, and since Marguerite Norris was the president of the team, she became the first woman ever to have her name engraved on the Stanley Cup. Seven other women have since had their names engraved on the trophy.

Canadian Women Dominate the Game

While Canada's hockey world waxes and wanes on the success and defeats of the men's national team, a group of women have been tearing up the international scene since they first formed in 1990. The women have won seven World Championship titles and have recently added a second Olympic gold medal to their trophy shelf, beating the U.S. team in 2002 and the Swedish team in 2006. But they are definitely not finished. Along with veterans like Hayley Wickenheiser and Cassie Campbell, a whole new group of talented young women are writing their own futures so that the Canadian women can hold on to the title as the best female hockey players in the world.

Chapter Six

THE MEN BEHIND THE MASK

A Different Breed

Since the first person put on the pads and stood in front of the net, it has been widely known that it takes a special breed to willingly place themselves in the path of a frozen rubber disc travelling at incredible speeds. The risks these players face in each practice and every game set them apart from their teammates, and the majority are blessed with a set of peculiarities that have defined goaltenders since the first stepped in front of a net. They not only risk bodily harm on the ice but also the wrath of the fans every time they let in a goal. They can make all the brilliant saves in the world, but if they let in that one goal that causes the team to lose, they are the first to hear of their mistakes. It is a thankless position sometimes, but most goaltenders wouldn't trade it for the world.

Jacques Plante best defined the plight of the goaltender: "How would you like it in your job if every time you made a mistake, a red light went on over your desk and 15,000 people stood up and yelled at you?"

The Best Behind the Mask

Terry Sawchuk

- One of the best goaltenders of all time, Terry Sawchuk played every game like it was overtime in game seven of the Stanley Cup playoffs.

- In his rookie season with the Detroit Red Wings (1950–51), he amassed an incredible 12 shutouts and a goals against average of 1.90, earning him the Calder Trophy as the NHL's best rookie.

- Sawchuk finished off the 1952 playoffs with a record 0.62 goals against average and won eight straight games to claim his first Stanley Cup.

- Sawchuk left the league with 104 career shutouts and 447 wins, a record that will be very hard to match.

- Sawchuk died tragically in 1970 as a result of injuries sustained in an altercation with his roommate.

Patrick Roy

- In his rookie season with Montréal, Roy lead the Canadiens through the rounds of the 1986 playoffs all the way to the Stanley Cup championship. His amazing performance earned him the Conn Smythe Trophy for the playoffs' most valuable player, his first of three such awards.

- He won the Cup again with the Canadiens in 1993 but was eventually traded because of a falling-out with Canadiens management.

- Roy found his way to the Colorado Avalanche, where he found immediate success, winning his third Stanley Cup in 1996 and his fourth in 2001.

- Patrick Roy officially announced his retirement in May 2004, ending his career with a record 551 wins, a career playoff win record of 151 and countless trophies and awards.

Georges Vezina

- Famed Montréal goaltender Georges Vezina was the first goaltender for the Montréal Canadiens franchise when it debuted in the National Hockey Association in 1910.

- Vezina finished the 1923–24 season with a 1.97 goals against average (the first under 2.00 in NHL history).

- Vezina turned away an incredible 78 shots in the first game of the playoffs against the Ottawa Senators for a 1–0 shutout victory. He then led the Canadiens into the two Stanley Cup series finals against Vancouver and Calgary, easily beating both teams to win the team's first Stanley Cup in the National Hockey League.

- Vezina had improved his regular season goals against average to 1.81 and was the first goaltender in Montréal history to win 100 career NHL games in 1924–25.

- On November 28, 1925, Vezina suited up to play against the Pittsburgh Pirates with a 102° fever and still stopped every single puck in the first period. He tried to play in the second period but collapsed on the ice. Five months later, Vezina died from complications due to tuberculosis in his hometown of Chicoutimi.

- The next season, the Canadiens donated the Vezina Trophy, given to the top NHL goalie in honour of a great man and his incredible goaltending legacy.

Vladislav Tretiak

- Although he never played a single game in the NHL, Vladislav Tretiak had a profound impact on hockey and how goaltenders play the game.

- Playing with the Soviet Central Red Army, Tretiak won three Olympic gold medals, one Olympic silver medal and 10 World Championship titles.

- Tretiak made a name for himself when he surprised the world with his goaltending skills during the 1972 Canada versus USSR Summit Series. Until Paul Henderson scored the winning goal, it was Tretiak who was the story of the series.

- Tretiak retired after the Soviets refused to let him join the NHL.

- He ended his career with an amazing international goals against average of 1.78 and was inducted into the Hockey Hall of Fame—the only non-NHL Russian player in the hall.

Ken Dryden

- With one of the most impressive goaltending resumes in the NHL, in just eight years with the Montréal Canadiens Ken Dryden won the Stanley Cup six times, was awarded five Vezina Trophies, played in five all-star games and received the Conn Smythe and Calder Trophy once each.

- The Boston Bruins originally drafted Dryden but gave his rights up for two players who never made any impact in the NHL.

- In his rookie year, he helped the Canadiens beat the defending champion Boston Bruins in the first round and go on to beat the Minnesota North Stars and the Chicago Blackhawks for his first of six Stanley Cups.

- For another eight seasons, Dryden backstopped the Habs to five more Stanley Cups and helped the Canadian National Team defeat the Russians in the 1972 Summit Series.

- With all his accomplishments, Dryden decided to leave the game after just eight seasons to pursue his career in law. Dryden was elected into the Hockey Hall of Fame in 1983.

Jacques Plante

- He won six Stanley Cups with the Canadiens, captured a record seven Vezina Trophies and was named to the all-star game eight times.

- Plante was one of the best goaltenders to ever play in the NHL, but he will always be remembered as the goaltender who first wore a mask on a regular basis.

- He first decided to wear the mask in a game after he was hit in the nose off an Andy Bathgate shot on November 1, 1959. He was said to have been the happiest guy ever to be hit in the face with a puck because it gave him the opportunity to wear the mask in a game.

- The Canadiens traded Plante to the Rangers just one year after he'd won the Vezina and Hart Trophies, but he only spent two seasons with the Rangers before retiring in 1965.

- When the league expanded in 1967, Plante was convinced to join the St. Louis Blues. In 1968, at the age of 39, Plante posted a 1.96 goals against average and won himself another Vezina Trophy.

Glenn Hall

- He was nicknamed "Mr. Goalie" for his dedication to the game and the toughest position on the ice.

- Hall won the Stanley Cup twice, the Vezina Trophy three times and was named to 13 all-star games.

- Hall played a record 551 consecutive games (including playoffs), a record that is likely to go unbeaten. His streak ended when he pulled a muscle in his back while tying his shoe.

- He is widely credited as having popularized and perfected the art of the butterfly style of goaltending.

- Mr.Goalie played for the Detroit Red Wings, the Chicago Blackhawks and the St. Louis Blues.

- He ended his career in 1971 after playing 906 games with 407 wins, 326 losses and 163 ties.

- Glenn Hall was inducted into the Hockey Hall of Fame in 1975.

Martin Brodeur

- Martin Brodeur is one of the best goaltenders playing today. He has earned three Stanley Cups with the New Jersey Devils, won Olympic gold for Canada and is the youngest goalie to reach the 300-win mark.

- Brodeur plays in a style that resembles the old stand-up goaltenders from the pre-expansion days, but he can switch gears easily and use the more common butterfly style that most net-minders use today.

- He can handle the puck extremely well and can make pinpoint passes out of his zone for offensive rushes. Just the knowledge that someone in their zone can handle the puck gives defence-men that extra edge over the competition.

- Brodeur has played remarkably well in nets for Canada's national men's hockey team, bringing home a World Championship title and helping to win Canada's first Olympic gold medal in 50 years at the 2002 Winter Olympic Games in Salt Lake City.

- He led the Devils to three Stanley Cups in 1995, 2000 and 2003. New Jersey's championships would have been almost impossible without Brodeur standing on his head in some of the series to keep his team alive.

- If all goes well for the goaltender, he will eventually challenge Patrick Roy's career record wins of 551. He recently passed Jacques Plante on the all-time wins list with 448 career wins.

Ed Belfour
- Belfour has won the Stanley Cup once with the Dallas Stars.

- He won the Calder Trophy in his rookie year.

- Belfour also won the Vezina Trophy twice and the William Jennings Trophy three times.

- He currently stands second on the all-time wins list with 457 wins.

- Belfour is one of only six goaltenders to post multiple 40-win seasons, along with Terry Sawchuk, Martin Brodeur, Bernie Parent, Ken Dryden and Jacques Plante.

- He is one of only two goaltenders with both a Stanley Cup and an Olympic gold medal to his credit—the other is Martin Brodeur.

Bernie Parent

- This flamboyant and outspoken goaltender won two consecutive Stanley Cups with the Philadelphia Flyers and became the only goaltender to take home two consecutive Conn Smythe trophies.

- He posted a record 47 wins in 1973–74.

- Parent is one of seven goaltenders in NHL history to post double-digit numbers in shutouts in consecutive seasons.

- He was the first-ever player signed by the World Hockey Association.

- Parent's number one sweater has now been retired by the Philadelphia Flyers.

The Physically Ill Goaltender

"Mr. Goalie" Glenn Hall, the man known for developing the butterfly style of goaltending who played in 503 consecutive games, often referred to goaltending as "60 minutes of hell." He loved playing the game, but he would get nervous to the point where he would vomit before most games. The nights he didn't toss his cookies were usually the ones that ended in defeat.

"I always felt I played better if I was physically sick before the game. If I wasn't sick, I felt I hadn't done everything I could to try to win," said Hall.

The Birth of the Face Mask

Although Jacques Plante is widely credited with the invention of the goalie's face mask, almost 30 years earlier, another goaltender was the first to play a professional game with facial protection.

On January 7, 1930, Montréal Maroons goaltender Clint Benedict took a Howie Morenz shot to the nose and cheekbone. Benedict had broken his nose this way many times before, and this time he decided to fashion a crude leather facemask to protect his nose in case he got another shot in the face. But the mask wasn't enough to protect him completely, and after he received another shot that broke his nose again, Benedict retired from the game. A goalie wearing a mask was not seen in the NHL until Jacques Plante came along and changed everything for good.

On November 1, 1959, after receiving a backhander off the face that opened up a large cut, Plante put on a facemask that he had been using only in practice. For the rest of the season and for the rest of his career, Plante played the position with what today is an essential part of the netminder's equipment.

Billy Smith's Goal

On November 28, 1979, the New York Islanders' Billy Smith was credited for something he didn't do and had his name put in the history books for becoming the first-ever NHL goaltender to be credited with a goal.

The never before seen but much talked-about "goaltender's goal" had been a myth, something goaltenders used to joke about in the confines of the dressing room. Never in the history of the NHL had a goaltender been credited with a goal until Smith came along.

The strange sequence of events all started when the Colorado Rockies took out their goaltender in favour of an extra attacker when the puck was in the Islanders zone. As the last person to touch the puck before Colorado's Rob Ramage shot the puck into his own empty net, Islanders goaltender Billy Smith was awarded the goal. Billy Smith smiled after the game, knowing that stats men across the league had to put a new column in the goaltender statistics that would show total goals for the season.

The First Real Goaltender's Goal

The first NHL goaltender to actually physically shoot the puck into the opposing team's net was the Philadelphia Flyers' Ron Hextall. His goal came when he chipped a shot down into the empty Boston Bruins cage on December 8, 1987. Hextall became the first goaltender to register 2 career goals when he scored another empty-net goal in the playoffs against the Washington Capitals on April 11, 1989, although this time the netminder purposely aimed a shot into the middle of the net.

However, the first time a goaltender was credited with a goal happened back on February 18, 1905, when Fred Brophy of the Montréal Westmounts made his way down to the other net and put the puck past Québec City netminder Paddy Moran.

Sawchuk's Many Trips to the Doctors

Terry Sawchuk will always be known as one of the greatest goaltenders ever to put on a pair of goalie pads, but he also has the dubious distinction of being one of the most bandaged netminders ever.

To know what kind of goaltender Terry Sawchuk was, just look at the photo from the March 4, 1966 edition of *Life* magazine. In the pages of the magazine, there is a close-up portrait of Sawchuk and the approximately 400 stitches he had received during his career as a netminder. Although the scars were enhanced with makeup for visual effect, each of the 400 stitches tells the story of all the pucks, sticks, skates and errant fists that found their way onto Sawchuk's face and of the man who was determined, no matter what the cost, to stop every shot that came his way.

Part of his success—and part of the reason why he had so many scars—was his style in the nets. By crouching low with his glove and blocker at the ready, Sawchuk was able to get a better view of the ice, allowing him to make quick-reaction saves and lateral moves much faster than a stand-up goaltender. His focus and intensity on the ice was legendary.

Penalty Box

Terry Sawchuk played hockey during a time when teams did not have a backup goaltender, requiring a special type of tough guy to stand in the crease. Once, after taking a puck in his face and lying on the ice unconscious, Sawchuk went to the dressing room, received his stitches and returned to play in the game. They just don't make them like they used to.

Last Place Team, First Place Goaltender

When the NHL awards are handed out at the end of the season, sometimes they are given to players who might not be on the Stanley Cup–winning team or have won any scoring championship but have made a significant impact on their team. When

Al Rollins of the 1954 Chicago Blackhawks was chosen as the recipient of the Hart Trophy as the league's most valuable player, everyone was caught off guard that the goaltender with a 12–47–7 record could be chosen as the league's MVP.

The 1953–54 season was a pitiful one for the Chicago Blackhawks. They struggled in every game they played, especially against the top two teams, Detroit and Montréal. Goaltender Al Rollins had the unsavoury job of guarding the nets for the lamentable Hawks and did his best to keep his team in the game every night but to no avail. The netminder tallied a regular-season record of 213 goals against at an average of 3.23 goals per game. When the all-star game players were named, Rollins was overlooked in favour of Toronto's Harry Lumley and Detroit's Terry Sawchuk. But as voting time came around at the end of the season, the voters thought that Rollins deserved a nod for his efforts in goal when the team in front of him was obviously so bad. The voters felt the Blackhawks would have been even worse without Rollins in goal.

Brother versus Brother

In the history of the National Hockey League, there have been many instances of brothers playing on the same team and even competing against each other as forwards or defencemen. But never had two brothers been pitted against each other as goaltenders until 1971, when Canadiens rookie netminder Ken Dryden went up against his brother Dave Dryden of the Buffalo Sabres. It was a match-up that almost didn't happen.

Ken Dryden had just been called up to the Cana-diens and noted that there was an upcoming game against his brother. Habs coach Al MacNeil had told him that he probably would not get the start, opting instead for veteran Rogie Vachon. But all that changed when Rogie Vachon went down in the sec-ond period with an injury. When Vachon didn't get up, Ken realized that he would be playing against Dave in only his third NHL game. For the first time since they were kids, the Dryden brothers played in a game against each other.

In his bestselling book, *The Game*, Ken Dryden admitted that he didn't like having his brother at the other end of the ice. "I didn't enjoy that game very much…Seeing Dave in the other goal was a distrac-tion I didn't want or need." Although he never voiced it, his brother Dave felt the same way at the other end of the ice, letting in the first shot on net on a 70-foot attempt by the Canadiens' Jacques Lemaire.

Montréal won the game 5–2, but the fans were more interested in the brothers on the ice than the final score. When the final buzzer sounded, Dave Dryden waited patiently at centre ice for his little brother. The pair gave each other a big smile and shook hands to the delight of the cheering crowd.

Brian Boucher's Shutout Streak

On New Year's Eve 2003, goaltender Brian Boucher recorded his first shutout against the Los Angeles Kings with a score of 4–0. It was a very good result for a goaltender who had been riding the pine since he entered the league in 1999, both with Philadelphia and his 2003–04 team, the Phoenix Coyotes. He continued his great goaltending with shutouts against the Dallas Stars, the Carolina Hurricanes, the Washington Capitals and the Minnesota Wild. The string ended in his next game against the Atlanta Thrashers. They scored at 6:16 of the first period, breaking his streak of 146 consecutive saves.

"It was a nice run, something that I'll never forget," said Boucher after the game. "But I think it's good for the team that we don't have to answer questions about it anymore."

It's a record that Boucher will cherish for the rest of his life, but his amazing feat of five consecutive games without allowing a single goal is only a modern-day record.

In hockey stats, "modern day" designates everything after the 1943–44 season (turn to "The Ever-Changing Rules of the Game" to find out why). The old-time record belongs to Alex Connell of the 1928 Ottawa Senators, who recorded an incredible six consecutive games without allowing a goal.

Very Heavy Workload

On an average night, a goaltender might face some 30 shots if his team is not playing well in front of him, but there have been many occasions when a goaltender had to perform above the norm and come to his team's rescue.

The modern-day record for the most saves in one regular season game goes to Ron Tugnutt of the 1991 Québec Nordiques. In a game against the Boston Bruins, poor little Tugnutt was left to his own devices to stop 70 of 73 shots in a 3–3 tie after overtime solved nothing. The crowd at the Boston Garden gave the Nordiques goalie a standing ovation for his heroic efforts in nets.

In the early days of hockey, the stats for shots on goal were not kept properly, and sometimes if the shot was directed at the net but missed, it still counted as a shot. So goaltenders like Lorne Chabot and Georges Vezina might have recorded shot totals of more than 70, but they didn't save all of them.

Goaltending for the Record Books

Most career shutouts: Terry Sawchuk's 103 career shutouts is one of the most difficult records for a modern-day goaltender to beat. Georges Hainsworth comes in second with 94 shutouts, followed by Glenn Hall in third with 84.

Most career wins: Patrick Roy crushed Terry Sawchuk's record of 447 career wins by more than 100 games. His 551 wins in 1029 games made him one of the most consistent goaltenders around. With Patrick Roy in nets, both the Montréal Canadiens and the Colorado Avalanche never went below .500 (winning percentage).

Most shutouts in one season: Hall of Fame goaltender Georges Hainsworth's record of 22 shutouts in just 44 games during the 1928–29 season will most likely never be matched, even with an 84-game schedule in today's regular NHL season. That year, Hainsworth led the Canadiens to a 22–7–15 record.

Most points scored in a career: Not your typical statistic for goaltenders, but Tom Barrasso scored 48 assists in his 19-year career, a record not easy to achieve. Grant Fuhr comes in second with 46 assists.

Most career playoff wins: Patrick Roy again holds the title with 148 wins. In his entire career, he only missed the playoffs once, with the Montréal Canadiens in the 1994–95 season. In each of his runs to the Stanley Cup, Roy recorded at least 15 wins.

Lowest career goals against average: It's a tie between Alex Connell and Georges Hainsworth at 1.91 goals per game. It must be noted that both goaltenders were playing during a time in the league when no forward passing was allowed and other rules heavily favoured the goalies. Today, it is considered quite the accomplishment if a goaltender can keep his stats below 2.00 goals per game.

First shutout in NHL history: Although there were just three goaltenders playing for three teams, the Montréal Canadiens Georges Vezina recorded the first-ever shutout in NHL history. The groundbreaking feat occurred on February 18, 1918, in a game against the Toronto Arenas in just the third month of the NHL's existence. The final score was a lopsided 9–0.

Chapter Seven

TOUPEES, SOILED CUPS AND OTHER ODD HAPPENINGS

What's that Under Hull's Rug?

Early in his career, Bobby Hull was known for two things: his amazing offensive talent on the ice and his golden hair that flowed gracefully in the air as he sped down the ice to score one of his many goals. With his chiselled good looks, the "Golden Jet" poster boy for the NHL was extremely sensitive about his hair, especially when it started to fall out. Unable to accept losing his hair, Hull became the first player in NHL history to wear a toupee.

Of course every player in the NHL knew Hull wore a hairpiece, but no one was foolish enough to mess the Golden One's new do. Hull was not one to shy away from a challenge, and he had 15-inch biceps to back him up. But curiosity won out for Steve Durbano, who played for the Birmingham Bulls of the (now defunct) World Hockey Association. On April 14, 1978, during a playoff game versus the Winnipeg Jets, Durbano decided to have a look under Hull's rug.

A fight broke out in the corner of the rink and several players were distracted, pulling players off each other. Durbano skated up behind Hull, who was preoccupied with another player, and ripped off the toupee, exposing Hull's bald head for everyone to see. Too embarrassed to pursue his exposer or his hairpiece, Hull rushed to the dressing room and returned to action wearing a helmet on his head and several shades of red on his face.

Penalty Box

Dave Hanson, famous for the role he played in the movie *Slapshot*, also stakes a claim to having been the one to have ripped Hull's hairpiece off, a strange title to battle over.

Strangely enough, no one knows or is saying what happened to the purloined hairpiece after it was torn from Hull's scalp.

Things You Don't Want In Your Stanley Cup

When you were a kid, your mother would always tell you not to put things into your mouth because you never knew where they had been. This sound advice should be taken into consideration by the next team to win the Cup, as many things have found their way into the bowl that had no business being there.

Stanley Cup Planter: Starting with the earliest alternative use for the Cup other than champagne and other beverages, the Stanley Cup was taken to a photographer's studio for a photo shoot and was mistakenly left behind. When the team didn't reclaim it, the photographer's wife used it to plant her favourite flowers. Luckily, someone figured out that the Cup was missing and rescued it from its flowerpot duties on the photographer's sunny windowsill.

The Porcelain Cup: Another foreign substance found its way into the Stanley Cup in 1937, after the Red Wings won the championship. During the celebrations, after consuming copious amounts of alcohol, Red Wing forward Gord Pettinger mistook the trophy for a toilet and urinated in the Cup. Hockey mythology also says that the same thing occurred after the Rangers Stanley Cup victory in 1940, but this time, the entire team used the Cup as their personal toilet.

The Stanley Cup Curse: Many fans and hockey players refer to the Stanley Cup as the Holy Grail of hockey and consider any defilement of the Cup as a sacrilege that risks a curse being placed on the team. The New York Rangers are firm believers in this curse. Not only did they use the Cup as their personal toilet after the 1940 victory, but Rangers president John Kilpatrick also burned the deed to the fully paid mortgage on Madison Square Garden in the bowl of the Cup. Legend says that a curse was placed on the team. It was another 54 years before the team saw the

Stanley Cup again. Whether they're believers or not, most players are certain it's best not to mess with the hockey gods.

Why Babies and Stanley Don't Mix: The most dubious of all the stories about foreign materials finding their way into the Cup would have to be when the Leafs won the championship in 1964 and Red Kelley got his turn with the Cup for a day. At the Kelley home, a photographer showed up to take pictures of the family happily surrounded by the Cup. Posing for one photo, Kelley decided it would make a really cute picture and a great family memento if he placed his infant son in the bowl for the shot. The picture was a wonderful memory, but his infant son, who was not wearing his diaper for the photo shoot, left behind some memories of his own. "He did the whole load in the Cup. He did everything," said Kelly. "That's why our family always laughs when we see players drinking champagne from the Cup."

Penalty Box

Here's another reason to think twice before taking that sip of champagne from the Cup. When the Detroit Red Wings won the championship in 1997, captain Steve Yzerman did not want to part company with the trophy and decided to take Lord Stanley's Cup into the shower with him.

Have Cup Will Travel

As more and more players from around the world compete and win the right to hold the Stanley Cup, the tradition of letting each player spend some quality time with it has resulted in a fair amount of travel for the piece of silverware. In the past 10 years alone, the Cup has travelled an estimated distance of over one million kilometres. Lord Stanley's Cup has travelled to almost every part of Canada, all across the United States, to a handful of cities in Eastern and Western Europe and even to Moscow's famous Red Square. The 1994 New York Rangers took it to a strip club, it was in a helicopter flown by Guy Lafleur, it was in an igloo in the Canadian north, it has been to the top of several mountains and to the bottom of several pools and was honoured by several Canadian prime ministers and American presidents. The keeper of the Cup, Walter Neubrand, has certainly earned every single air mile.

Against All Odds: A Deaf Hockey Player

Over the years, the NHL has seen many remarkable achievements by its players and the people that surround them, but no one had ever seen the likes of Jim Kyte when he joined the league in 1983 as the only deaf hockey player to play for an NHL team.

Kyte was the perfect stay-at-home defenceman. With his six-foot-five frame and 210 pounds, he could clear any opponent out of his goaltender's crease. Legally deaf, his hearing did limit his performance on the ice at times, but nothing that created any serious problems. Not able to hear the whistle on an offside or icing call, Kyte often continued battling in the corner with a confused opponent. He did wear a hearing aid to help boost the little hearing that he did have, but in the noise of the arena, Kyte had to rely on his instincts most of the time.

"When I was in junior, one guy used to call me 'Radio Shack' all the time," said Kyte, laughing off the ribbing from his teammates.

After his years with the Winnipeg Jets, Kyte spent several years bouncing around teams before settling with the San Jose Sharks. He retired in 1996 after 13 successful years in the NHL.

Step Aside, Mr. Cheevers

It's not normally something that a professional goaltender would do during a game, but Gerry Cheevers, who played for the Boston Bruins in the late '60s and '70s, wasn't your run-of-the-mill professional goaltender.

Most famous for his goalie's mask that had stitches painted all over it, Cheevers was also known as a bit of a joker on and off the ice. One of Cheevers' most memorable moments came during a game against the Chicago Blackhawks. The incident involved the Blackhawks' Bobby Hull, who was known for his wicked slap shot and his penchant for whizzing the puck ever so close to goaltenders' heads.

The Bruins and Cheevers were not having a good game, and the Blackhawks were ahead by 4 goals late into the third period. With little time left in the period, Bobby Hull got hold of the puck.

Just before shooting, Hull looked up at the last second to see the remaining defenceman with his stick out and his eyes firmly shut. Cheevers was hiding behind the defenceman to shield himself from the shot, leaving the net completely open. Hull was just able to get the shot into the net before breaking into laughter. Hull asked Cheevers why he let him have the open net. Cheevers simply replied, "I'm crazy, but not that crazy."

The Invention of the Puck

There are many legends about how the first puck came into existence, but one of the most famous comes from the 1860s, when two teams were playing a game at Montréal's Victoria skating rink. The "puck" in those early days was actually a solid ball of bouncy rubber like the one used in a lacrosse game. During the game, the players whacked at the "puck," and it bounced in every direction and flew over the low boards that had been set up to protect the onlookers, smashing several of the arena's windows before the destructive little "puck" could be captured.

Annoyed by the destruction of his windows and the expense of having them replaced, the rink manager grabbed the "puck," took a sharp knife and cut off the top and bottom sections of the rubber ball, leaving only the flat centre section. The players noticed that the new flat "puck" slid along the ice more easily, and even better, no more windows were smashed.

The Only Puck to Last through a Game

In every NHL game, there is a bucket of pucks on standby for the referees and linemen to use in case one goes flying into the crowd or splits in two after a hard slap shot off the goalpost. Only once in NHL history has one puck been used for an entire game. On November 10, 1979, the Los Angeles Kings and the Minnesota North Stars played an entire game with just one puck. The puck, which is now immortalized in the Hockey Hall of Fame, never left the ice surface for the entire game, and despite a few missing chunks, could actually still be used.

Penalty Box

Back in the early days of the NHL, pucks were not as readily available as they are today. For most games, only two pucks were used, one for the game and one for emergencies. When a puck flew into the crowd, a fan would throw it back onto the ice, or else the game could be cancelled.

The word "puck" comes from the Irish game of hurling. "To puck" referred to the act of hitting the ball with a stick. A puck is also an evil spirit or a mischievous sprite or hobgoblin. Puck is also a satellite of the planet Uranus.

Here Come the Hats

The tradition of throwing hats onto the ice after a player scores 3 goals hasn't always been part of the game. Before 1946, scoring 3 goals was called just that, 3 goals, and not a "hat trick," as it is more commonly known today. The term came about in 1946, when fashionable Chicago Blackhawks forward Alex Kaleta walked into a local haberdashery in Toronto owned by Sammy Taft. Kaleta bet the hatter that if he scored 3 goals in the game that night against the Maple Leafs, Taft would have to give him a hat of his choice for free. Knowing that scoring 3 goals was quite unlikely, Taft took the young Blackhawks forward's bet. Kaleta scored his 3 goals that night and walked into Taft's hat store the next day to collect his winnings. The newspapers got wind of the story and quoted Taft saying, "Yeah, that was some trick he pulled to get that hat." The feat became known from that day on as a "hat trick." Ever the smart businessman, Taft used the publicity from the Kaleta story to promote his business. Every time a Toronto player scored 3 goals he would give him a free hat. The term has stuck ever since, and now the crowd supplies the hats for the players by throwing them on the ice after a hat trick.

The Death of "Bad" Joe Hall

Most people remember that the Stanley Cup was not awarded in the 1919 series between the Montréal Canadiens and the Seattle Metropolitans because of the Spanish influenza outbreak, but few remember the name of the only player to die from the disease.

"Bad" Joe Hall was an effective defenceman for the Canadiens during the 1918–19 regular season, and he was instrumental in helping the Canadiens make it to the Stanley Cup finals against the Seattle Metropolitans. But all would take a turn for the worse in game five, when Hall was on the ice for a shift and clearly had difficulty skating. When the whistle stopped the play, Hall skated over to the bench and was immediately taken to the local hospital. It was confirmed that the tough defenceman had contracted the influenza virus. Several other players joined him in hospital, and the Cup was cancelled for fear that more might fall ill. Six days later, Hall died in the hospital. Montréal Canadiens owner Georges Kennedy also died from the complications of the disease over a year later.

Banned For Life

Billy Coutu wasn't the best player in the NHL, but he was a solid defenceman who could be relied on when things got a little rough in the corners. He played for the Hamilton Tigers and the Montréal Canadiens before being traded to the Boston Bruins at the start of the 1926 regular season.

Coutu started off his career with the Bruins on a bad note when during his first practice he took offence at some good-natured ribbing from his defensive partner, Eddie Shore, and body-slammed him into the ice, severing Shore's ear during the collision.

Coutu continued his bad ways. In game four of the 1927 Stanley Cup finals between the Bruins and the Ottawa Senators, he started a brawl at the request of coach Art Ross. During the altercation, Coutu ended up punching referee Jerry Laflamme and was suspended from the National Hockey League for life, becoming the first-ever player to receive the dishonour—but not the last.

Bad Luck Coach

All coaches go through some bad times with their teams. Losing is simply part of the game, but you have to feel sorry for one coach in particular who lost in 12 Stanley Cup finals.

Dick Irvin was one of the greatest coaches in NHL history, but he had some bad luck when it came to the Stanley Cup finals. Although he did win the Cup four times and had an overall record of 692 wins and 527 losses (coaching Toronto and Montréal), Irvin was just unlucky when it came to the finals. But you at least have to give the man credit for making it to the finals so many times.

Eddie Shore Ends Bailey's Career

Those who think violence in hockey is new just have to look in the hockey history books to find plenty of examples of on-ice aggression. One of the first violent incidents in the NHL occurred during a December 1933 game between the Boston Bruins and the Toronto Maple Leafs.

During the game, Boston enforcer Eddie Shore was up to his usual antics when King Clancy decided to get even with the unsuspecting player, tripping the Bruin when he wasn't looking. Shore looked at the referee to see if a penalty had been called on the obvious trip, but the referee either missed the play or decided that Toronto was just getting back at Shore for some of his infractions and let the play continue.

Enraged that no penalty had been called, Shore scanned the Leafs players, looking for his aggressor. The first Leafs jersey he happened to see was Ace Bailey's. Shore delivered a vicious crosscheck from behind, sending Bailey through the air.

Knocked senseless, Bailey hit the ice, his bare head taking the worst of the impact. The crowd and the players went silent as Bailey's legs twitched wildly. After seeing what Shore had just done, Toronto defenceman Red Horner paid Shore back with one punch that sent him down to the ice with a large cut on his forehead.

Doctors rushed the critically injured Bailey to the nearest hospital, where neurosurgeons cleared the blood clot from his brain after two lengthy surgeries. Bailey recovered from his injuries, but he never played another game in the National Hockey League.

The First Hall of Famer to Die in World War I

World War I denied many young men a successful future, but none were missed more on the ice than the almost-mythical talent of Frank McGee, who became the first Hall of Fame member to die in World War I. With the Ottawa Silver Seven, McGee helped his team to three consecutive Stanley Cup victories from 1903 to 1905 and assured his place among hockey's greatest when he scored a record 14 goals in one Stanley Cup game. He continued to impress when he scored 28 goals in seven games during the following season. All these stats are even more incredible when you consider that McGee was only able to see through one eye because of an injury he suffered playing hockey.

Although he retired from the sport in 1907, McGee still had some fight left in him, and he joined the army in 1916 to fight in World War I. The army did not normally accept one-eyed applicants, but being the nephew of Thomas D'Arcy McGee certainly helped.

McGee served Canada proudly, but tragically, he lost his life defending his country during the Battle of the Somme on September 16, 1916.

Played for Team and Died for Country

Dudley Garrett only played 23 games for the New York Rangers during the 1942–43 season before the Canadian government came calling, sending him off to World War II. The navy man was just off the coast of Newfoundland on a Canadian ship when it went down, killing Garrett on November 25, 1945.

A one-time goaltender for the Detroit Red Wings, Joseph Turner also lost his life during the war when he was killed in action in Holland on January 12, 1945, although his death was not recorded until December 19 that same year.

The Tragic End of Howie Morenz

The Babe Ruth of Hockey, Howie Morenz was the Montréal Canadiens' and hockey's first superstar. Between 1923 and 1933, Morenz led the Canadiens to three Stanley Cups, won three Hart Trophies as the NHL's most valuable player and took home two Art Ross Trophies as the NHL top scorer. But by 1934, his touch seemed to fade into memory, and the Canadiens traded the aging superstar to the Chicago Blackhawks. After two unsuccessful seasons with the Hawks and a brief stay with the New York Rangers, Morenz returned to the town that made him a superstar. But it all came crashing down in one fateful game against his old Chicago Blackhawks team.

In the first period, Morenz rushed into the corner after the puck. As he hit the boards, his skate got caught in a groove in the ice at the exact moment when Chicago defenceman Earl Siebert crashed into him from behind. Morenz twisted awkwardly, sending his body one way while his leg stayed locked between the ice and the boards. The crowd suddenly went silent as the crack from his breaking bones echoed through to every corner of the Forum.

When doctors delivered the news that he would never play again, Morenz sank deep into depression. After lying in bed for nearly a month, Morenz decided he'd had enough, and despite the cast on his leg, he was going to walk out of the hospital. On March 8, 1937, Morenz got out of the bed, took one step, fell to the floor and died. Doctors said he died from a cardiac deficiency, but friends and family knew that his death was at least partially caused by the fact that he could never again play the sport that he loved.

On March 11, 1937, 15,000 people jammed the Montréal Forum for Howie Morenz's funeral. Thousands more waited outside for their chance to file past the coffin and pay their final respects to the man who had given them so much.

The Amazing Player that Never Was

Bill Masterton only played 38 games in the National Hockey League, but his legacy would last forever. The tough centre's NHL career started off well when he scored the franchise's first goal on October 11, 1967. He wasn't one of the top-scoring forwards in the league, but his focus and dedication made him a perfect asset for the new franchise. He was headed for a long, successful career—until the night of January 13, 1968, when the North Stars faced off against the Oakland Seals.

As Masterton came to the Seals' blue line, the puck slipped off his stick and passed in between the two defencemen. When Masterson rushed in between the two players to go for a breakaway, they collided, sending Masterton flying into the air. He lost his balance and struck his head on the ice. Play was immediately stopped, and medics ran out onto the ice to tend to Masterton. He was rushed to hospital, but the damage to his brain was severe, and the swelling could not be controlled. He succumbed to his injuries and died in the hospital two days later.

His career was short-lived, but his passion for the game lived on. The NHL created the Bill Masterton Trophy the next year to be awarded to the player who best displays perseverance, sportsmanship and dedication to the game. The first winner of the trophy was Claude Provost of the Montréal Canadiens.

The Near-End of Clint Malarchuk

Buffalo Sabres goaltender Clint Malarchuk came close to losing his life on March 22, 1989, when St. Louis Blues forward Steve Tuttle collided with a Sabres defenceman and was sent flying through the air at Malarchuk. In the collision, Tuttle's skate sliced into Malarchuk's neck, severing his jugular vein. Were it not for the quick thinking of trainer Jim Pizzutelli, who slowed the loss of blood until doctors could operate, Malarchuk would have died that night.

McSorley Goes Out with His Head Down

Marty McSorley was always known as the tough guy on any team he played with. He ranks fourth in all-time penalty minutes and has seen his fair share of fights during his career. But the tough defenceman was never known for being a cheap-shot artist until the game on February 21, 2000, between McSorley's Boston Bruins and the Vancouver Canucks.

All game, McSorley and Canuck forward Donald Brashear had been at each other's throats, even fighting early on. As the game progressed, McSorley wanted to drop the gloves again, but the Canuck was having no part of McSorley's plans and skated away from him several times. McSorley shadowed him up the ice and then proceeded to give Brashear a two-handed smack to the temple with his stick. Brashear fell like a stone to the ice, smacking his head, while his body shook from the shock of the dangerous assault. The hit came with just three seconds remaining in the game. Paramedics immediately removed Brashear from the ice and took him to the hospital, where it was revealed that he had suffered a serious concussion.

McSorley was suspended indefinitely from the NHL, but a Vancouver judge handed out a more serious penalty. McSorley was found guilty of assault with a weapon and given 18 months probation for his crime. The indefinite suspension made McSorley just the second player in NHL history to be banned from the league.

Retribution, Bertuzzi Style!

The Vancouver Canucks were again involved in another black mark in the history of hockey in 2004 when Canucks forward Todd Bertuzzi decided to pay back Colorado's Steve Moore for an incident earlier in the season when Moore knocked out Canuck captain Markus Naslund with an open-ice shoulder hit to the head. The Canucks were upset that no penalty was called and that the league did nothing to Moore for his actions. Brad May put a bounty on Moore's head after the game for what he did to his captain.

Fast-forward to March 8, several weeks later, in Vancouver. With the Avalanche leading 8–2 in the middle of the third period, Bertuzzi saw his chance to get back at Moore. After following him up ice and attempting to get him to fight, Bertuzzi sucker-punched Moore from behind, knocking him to the ice. The crowd fell silent as the unconscious Moore was put on a stretcher and taken to the hospital, where doctors diagnosed him with a severe concussion and three broken vertebrae.

Two days after the incident, Todd Bertuzzi publicly apologized before a throng of reporters: "To the fans of hockey and the fans of Vancouver, to the kids that watch this game, I'm truly sorry. I don't play the game that way. I'm not a mean-spirited person. I'm sorry for what happened."

For his crime, Bertuzzi was suspended from the NHL for 17 months, and a Vancouver court convicted him of assault, with a one-year probation plus 80 hours of community service. Moore has not been able to return to the NHL, and he filed a multi-million-dollar lawsuit against Bertuzzi for damages and lost wages.

The Worst NHL Teams

The 1974–75 Washington Capitals

The worst modern-era team in the National Hockey League was, without a doubt, the Washington Capitals during the 1974–75 season. Although it was their first year in the NHL, the team had a terrible record of 8 wins, 67 losses and 5 ties for a pitiful points total of 21. Montréal, Buffalo and Philadelphia were tied with the most points at 113, and the second-lowest regular season point total that year came from the Kansas City Scouts, also a first-year expansion team with 41 points. Washington lost a record 17 games in a row (tied with San Jose) and at one point in the season had a 37-game winless streak on the road. The hapless Capitals lost 3 games by 10 or more goals, and by the end of the season, they had let in a record 446 goals against. Goaltenders Ron Low and Michel Belhumeur shared the unfortunate duty of tending the net every night and racked up a 5.4 goals per game average.

The 1980–81 Winnipeg Jets

Another victim of the expansion team blues was the Winnipeg Jets of the 1980–81 season. Like the 1974–75 Capitals, the Jets went through three coaches in one year and had a terrible run of 30 games without a win (23 losses and 7 ties). They won only 9 games all season and lost 57. But there was a silver lining to the horrible year—being dead last at the end of the regular season assured them the first choice overall in the NHL entry draft, which they used to select Dale Hawerchuk. The next season saw an incredible turnaround when they finished the season with a record of 33–33–14 and made it into the playoffs for the first time.

The 1992–93 Ottawa Senators

Expansion continued to be unkind to first-year clubs as the Ottawa Senators compiled a horrible record of 10–70–4 by the end of the 1992–93 regular season. The team started off the season on a high note, beating the Montréal Canadiens 5–3 in their home opener, but Ottawa only managed nine more wins the rest of the season. They were so bad that year that they went 38 games on the road without a victory. It would take a few more years to work the bugs out of the franchise, but Ottawa has rebounded to become one of the best teams in the NHL.

The 1919–20 Québec Bulldogs

They had one of the most prolific goal scorers in hockey history on their team, but the Québec Bulldogs could only manage four wins in the 1919–20 season. Leading scorer Joe Malone finished the season with 39 goals and 10 assists.

Malone also set the record for most goals by an individual in one game with 7. The Bulldogs folded at the end of the season and became the Hamilton Tigers, but the losing continued into the new season as the team won only six games in the 1920–21 season.

The 1992–93 San Jose Sharks

The first-year problems associated with expansion teams failed to pass by the San Jose Sharks, as they broke the record for most losses in one season with 71. San Jose's overall record for the year was a dismal 11–71–2, giving them just 24 points for the season. The 1993–94 season was a different story for the new team. They finished the regular season with a respectable 82 points and made it all the way to the conference semifinals, only to lose to the Toronto Maple Leafs in a hard-fought series that went seven games.

The 2005–06 Pittsburgh Penguins

Although many hockey pundits predicted that the Pittsburgh Penguins would be the team to watch before the start of the season with star players like rookie sensation and media darling Sidney Crosby, Mario Lemieux, Sergei Gonchar, Mark Recchi and John Leclair. But reality quickly set in, and the Penguins ended the season with the worst record in the NHL that season.

Chapter Nine

WHAT'S IN A NAME?

Famous Threesomes

It's a long-standing but strange tradition in hockey that when a right winger, centre, and left winger produce a steady stream of points, they are given a nickname that somehow fits their character and style of play. The modern hockey line of the NHL today rarely receives the honour of a nickname because so few of the lines are kept together long enough for sports media to give them one. With the increase in the number of players on the bench, coaches are now able to juggle their lines according to the rhythm of the game, opting on most lines to keep a pair together while switching the third player as necessary. So nowadays you just don't get those great nicknames of the past. Here are a few of the most famous hockey lines:

The Production Line—The Detroit Red Wings of the original-six era between 1949 and 1955 was one of the greatest teams to play the game. The Wings finished first in the league several times, had some of the best players on the team and won the Stanley Cup four times. One of the biggest reasons for their success was a trio of players who were dubbed the Production Line—Sid Abel, Gordie Howe and Ted Lindsay. The Production Line dominated every time they stepped on the ice. They were three big forwards who could skate and get back into their zone to cover on defence. Detroit manager Jack Adams and coach Tommy Ivan tried breaking up the line to spread the talent around, but the chemistry just wasn't there, and the big three were always put right back together. The Production Line had their best year in the 1949–50 season, when the three finished 1–2–3 in scoring at the end of the regular season, with Lindsay in first with 78 points, Abel with 69 and Howe right behind with 68. Just like a Detroit automobile factory, the Production Line kept producing until Abel was traded to the Chicago Blackhawks in 1952.

The Punch Line—Of all the great lines to play for the Montréal Canadiens, one of the best had Maurice Richard on right wing, Elmer Lach at centre and Hector Blake on left wing during the 1940s. The trio finished 1–2–3 in scoring during the 1944–45 season, with Lach in first with 80 points, Richard with his famous 50 goals and 73 points and Blake with 67 points. Lach was the set-up man to Richard's goal-scoring touch, and Blake backed them up with solid forechecking and an instinctive, defensive style of play. The line was responsible for some of the most exciting plays in hockey and laid the foundation for one of the best teams in NHL history. Blake would later return to Montréal after retiring from his on-ice duties and team up with Richard once again to coach the Habs to eight Stanley Cups in 13 seasons.

The Kraut Line—Milt Schmidt, Woody Dumart and Bobby Bauer were nicknamed the Kraut Line because all three players came from Kitchener, Ontario (formerly named Berlin), a town known for its German heritage. First put together on the same line for the 1938–39 season, the Kraut Line helped the Boston Bruins to their second Stanley Cup. In their second year as linemates, the trio led the league in scoring. Schmidt was in first with 52 points, Dumart was second with 43, and in third place was Bauer with 43 points as well. The Kraut Line shone again in the 1940–41 season, leading Boston to their third first-place regular season finish and their second Stanley Cup victory, beating the Detroit Red Wings in four straight games. The line was broken up when all three were called into military service for World War II, but the trio continued their on-ice antics on the military hockey team, dominating all hopeless challengers.

The French Connection—There have been many incarnations of the French Connection over the years but only one original—the '70s Buffalo Sabres trio of Gilbert Perreault, Richard Martin and Rene Robert. One of the most offensive trios of the time, the French Connection quickly helped the expansion Buffalo Sabres out of the basement and into the Stanley Cup finals by 1975. Richard Martin broke the 50-goal plateau two years in a row, and Perreault and Robert both broke the 100-point mark on several occasions. The trio continued racking up points until the end of the decade. Robert was traded to the Colorado Rockies in 1979 and Martin suffered a career-ending knee injury in 1980.

The Pony Line—One of the fastest lines of the '40s, the Chicago Blackhawks trio of Max Bentley, his brother Doug Bentley and Bill Mosienko were said to run like wild horses over defenders in their lust for scoring—hence the name Pony Line. The brothers from Delisle, Saskatchewan, and Winnipeger Mosienko were the lone bright spots on a Chicago squad that had seen better days, finishing near the bottom of the league several times and missing out on the playoffs all but twice in the line's time together. The shining moment came in the 1944 playoffs when they made it to the finals against the Montréal Canadiens, but they unfortunately lost in four straight games, unable to match Montréal's speed and the clutch goaltending of Bill Durnan.

The Long Island Lightning—The Long Island Lightning—Mike Bossy, Clark Gilles and Bryan Trottier—was the major offensive force behind the New York Islanders dynasty of the '80s, providing some of the most spectacular plays and record-breaking point totals. Led by the prodigious scoring talents of Mike Bossy, the line was part of one of the best all-round teams in the NHL.

The Smurf Line—While the line did not last long, and they really didn't put up big numbers, the trio of Saku Koivu, Oleg Petrov and Valeri Bure of the late '90s Montréal Canadiens was given the nickname of the Smurf Line because of their small stature. The trio did not last long, as many of the larger lines in the NHL easily dominated the smaller players on the ice.

Hockey's Most Famous and Infamous Nicknames

Maurice "the Rocket" Richard—When he first broke into the National Hockey League, Richard was close to being nicknamed after his brittle bones when he broke his leg in the minors and fractured his heel just a few games into his rookie season. All that was quickly forgotten once people got a glimpse of what he could do on the ice. A physical force, Richard could speed into his opponent's zone and be directly in front of the goaltender before any defencemen had a chance to react. It wasn't until two years later that he received his famous moniker. During a Montréal Canadiens practice, as Richard put himself through his usual difficult paces, a teammate yelled out as Richard sped by the bench, "Watch out, here comes the Rocket!" A newspaper reporter at the practice overheard the comment and published it in his next article. From then on, the name stuck.

King Clancy—During his prime, King Clancy was a star defenceman for the Ottawa Senators and the Toronto Maple Leafs from 1921 to 1936. The nickname suited his character perfectly. He was always at the centre of every battle and wasn't afraid to open his royal mouth to make his declarations heard. It's hard to believe that this flamboyant character's real name was Francis.

Boom Boom—Bernard Geoffrion earned his nickname for the simple reason that he could shoot the puck as hard as a cannon and check his opponents with equal force. He is often credited with perfecting the slap shot during a time when most players opted for wrist shots and quick snapshots. With linemates like Maurice Richard and Jean Beliveau, it wasn't easy to make a name for oneself in Montréal, but Boom Boom's fiery spirit and fierce attitude on the ice won him many fans wherever he went.

The Great One—Wayne Gretzky—61 NHL records held or shared, 894 career goals, 1963 career assists, 92 goals in one season, 215 points in one season, 50 goals in 39 games, four Stanley Cups, 18 all-star games, countless NHL trophies, etc. etc. etc… The nickname is self-explanatory.

The Golden Jet—Bobby Hull was hockey's golden boy. The perfect image of the NHL athlete: chiselled good looks, muscular physique and curly blond locks. His looks only enhanced the image of one of the fastest skaters of the time, who possessed a deadly slap shot and a scoring touch that lifted the Chicago Blackhawks out of the bottom of the league and into the Stanley Cup championship in 1961.

The Pocket Rocket—He will always be known as Maurice Richard's younger brother, but Henri Richard managed to make a name for himself with the Montréal Canadiens, winning 11 Stanley Cups over a remarkable career. He got the name Pocket Rocket because he played a similar game to his older brother, using his speed through the neutral zone and his natural instincts around the net to score goals, and he was several inches shorter than his brother as well.

Tiger—Dave "Tiger" Williams earned his moniker through sheer force and aggression. An average offensive player, Williams was noted more for his abilities with his gloves off and his verbal skills when taunting other players, referees, coaches and fans. He holds the dubious distinction of being the most penalized player in NHL history, with 3966 minutes of regular-season time served.

Punch—Noted mostly for his coaching duties with the Toronto Maple Leafs during their golden years between 1958 and 1969, Imlach earned his nickname long before his days behind the bench. During a game when Imlach played minor hockey, he was knocked out, and when he was taken to the dressing room, he took a punch at one of the trainers for having him taken off the ice.

Toe, or the Old Lamplighter—"Toe" Blake got his first nickname when his younger sister had trouble pronouncing his first name, Hector. He was called the Old Lamplighter because of his natural ability to put the puck in the net. Every time he did, the red light went on. He scored 235 goals in 577 career games, but it was his time as coach of the Montréal Canadiens that earned him his place in history for winning the Stanley Cup eight times.

Gump—Lorne Worsley was given the name Gump not because of any significant hockey moment in his career but from the simple fact that as a child he resembled the comic strip character Andy Gump. Gump Worsley spent 21 years as a goaltender in the National Hockey League, backstopping the Montréal Canadiens for four Stanley Cups in the '60s.

Mr. Hockey—Other than "The Great One," no other nickname sums up the character and career of a player than that of Gordie Howe, Mr. Hockey himself. He played professional hockey over six decades, amassed some of the most incredible statistics in the game, became an excellent ambassador for the game of hockey and is a role model for kids even today.

Although some players were better skaters or better scorers, no one on the ice could match Howe's intensity and remarkable consistency. Even into his 50s, Howe played all 80 season games and recorded a respectable 15 goals and 26 assists. Not bad for a grandfather.

Puck Goesinski—Unfortunately, some nicknames are given to players for something they would rather not be remembered for. That's the case with Steve "the Puck Goesinski" Buzinski. A goaltender for the New York Rangers in 1942, Buzinski only played nine games for the team, letting in an average of six goals per game. Steve "The Puck Goesinski" Buzinski never got another chance in the NHL.

In the Wrong Place at the Wrong Time Reece—Dave Reece's career lasted just 14 games with the Boston Bruins in the 1974–75 season. His unfortunate nickname came from one game when he was put in nets against the Toronto Maple Leafs. Leafs captain Daryl Sittler scored a record 6 goals and 4 assists for a 10-point game. After the game, Sittler tried to diffuse the press from coming down hard on the rookie goaltender, saying that most of the goals were not Reece's fault because he was either screened or they deflected off a defenceman. The media used this quote and dubbed the rookie Boston netminder "In the Wrong Place at the Wrong Time Reece." He never played another NHL game.

The Finnish Flash—Teemu Selanne is a rarity among players with nicknames. Most earn their names after years in the NHL, but Teemu was dubbed the Finnish Flash in just his first season. In his inaugural year with the Winnipeg Jets, Teemu scored 76 goals (a rookie record) and won the Calder Trophy for his exploits.

Saint Patrick—Saint Patrick is more commonly known outside the Montréal area as Patrick Roy. During his time with the Canadiens, he became a fan favourite after his many game-saving performances for Les Glorieux, to the point where many fans began to refer to him as Saint Patrick. What other name befits a goaltender who won the Canadiens two Stanley Cups and was their unofficial leader for 10 seasons?

Sid the Kid—Joining the NHL at the tender age of 18 will earn a player a great deal of respect but also a little friendly joking from fellow players. So when 18-year-old hockey phenom Sidney Crosby joined the Pittsburgh Penguins for the start of the 2005–06 season, he quickly became known as Sid the Kid, not just because of his age but also for his baby face. Hopefully as time passes, he can shed the nickname.

Chapter Ten

THE EVER-CHANGING RULES OF THE GAME

The Death of the Stand-Up Goaltender

Before the founding of the National Hockey League in 1917, the National Hockey Association was the major professional hockey league in North America. One of its hard and fast rules that got passed on to the NHL was that goaltenders could not fall to the ice to stop the puck. If the goalie intentionally fell to make the save, he was given a minor penalty.

One goaltender challenged this rule and changed the face of hockey forever. Clint Benedict, also known for being the first goalie to wear a mask, saw this rule as a restriction on how the position should be played. He knew goaltenders could cover a lot more of the net if they could fall to the ice to make the save. Benedict developed a strategy to avoiding the minor penalty by making his fall look accidental, making the referee think twice about awarding the other team a power play.

"What you had to be is sneaky," said Benedict, looking back to his early days. "You'd make a move, fake losing your balance or footing, and put the officials on the spot—did I fall down, or did I intentionally go down?"

He fell so often that newspapers dubbed Benedict "Tumbling Clint" and "Praying Benny" because he was on his knees so often. Referees, tired of having to decipher Benedict's acting, brought their complaints to NHL president Frank Calder during the 1917–18 season. Calder finally took the rule out of the official books on January 9, 1918.

"In the future, they [goaltenders] can fall on their knees, or stand on their heads, if they think they can stop the puck better in that way than standing on their feet," said Calder in an interview with the now-defunct *Montréal Star*.

"And the Teams are ready for the Opening Bully..."

Before the faceoff came into hockey, the system used to determine who would get control of the puck was known as the "bully." Most people know this procedure from the games of pick-up hockey they played as kids at the local rinks when referees weren't around to drop the puck. Two players would line up facing each other and tap their sticks three times before attempting to gain control of the puck. In 1900, referee Fred Waghorne instituted the modern faceoff that we still see today.

No Forward Passing

Before 1929, goaltenders ruled the NHL. In one season, Canadiens goalie Georges Hainsworth recorded 22 shutouts in 44 games. Defence was the name of the game in those days, since forward passing in the offensive zone was not allowed. The rules made it extremely difficult to enter into an opposing team's zone. Add to that the fact that teams were allowed to keep as many players as they wanted in the defensive zone, sending just one or two men on an offensive rush, in order to protect a lead. All this changed in 1929, when the league instituted a set of groundbreaking rules that would change the game forever.

To open up the game and increase the lagging forward stats, the NHL decided to allow forward passing and penalize a team that kept more than three players (including the goaltender) in the defensive zone while the play moved up the ice. The difference was immediate. Players' scoring percentages skyrocketed as goaltenders' save percentages plummeted. Just a year before that, Montréal Canadiens star forward Howie Morenz was in the top five of the regular scoring leaders with 17 goals in 42 games. The next year, with the new rules, Morenz's stats increased to 40 goals in 44 games. Goaltenders' stats also increased. Georges Hainsworth's amazing 0.92 goal average increased to 2.42 in just one season.

The Ultimate Power Play

Before the 1955–56 NHL season, when a player was assessed a minor penalty he had to sit his punishment out for the entire two minutes. This meant that the opposing team was free to score as many goals as it liked in that two-minute period. If it was on the power play, a team could really rebound or put themselves far out of reach of the other team by scoring 2 or 3 goals. The rule changed when the high-scoring Montréal Canadiens, at the beginning of their '50s dynasty, used the minor power play rule to their advantage.

The league decided to change the rule after one particular game on November 5, 1955, when the Canadiens played to a 4–2 victory over the Boston Bruins. After the Bruins were called for a two-minute minor penalty, scoring ace Jean Beliveau scored 3 times in 44 seconds, leaving many to question the minor penalty rule. At the end of the season, the less defensive teams in the league protested, and the rule was changed so that after a goal was scored during a minor penalty, the penalized team could return to full strength.

The Modern-Day Rule

Prior to the 1943–44 season, the NHL suffered from an ailment that continues to surface every so often in the league—low scoring. With many of the league's top players called off to war and most teams opting for a defensive strategy, the league needed to make some changes to keep people in the stands during the difficult war years.

In September 1943, the NHL board of governors met to find a solution to the lack of offence in the game. They unanimously voted to add a red line at centre ice. The main reason behind the change was to reduce the number of offside calls to encourage a more fluid approach to the game. From that season on, hockey was in the modern era.

Is that Your Toe in the Crease?

Goaltenders have always complained that they get no respect from other players in their crease, even though they are supposed to be free from any harassment inside the safety of their semicircle. So when the league announced before the start of the 1998–99 season that they would be cracking down with a zero-tolerance policy for players found in the crease when a goal was scored, goalies rejoiced.

What happened during the regular season was reviewed goal after reviewed goal after reviewed goal, slowing down the games and angering fans but pleasing goaltenders. At the end of the season, four netminders finished with goals-per-game averages of less than 2.00 for the first time since the 1931 season.

The league finally realized the error of its ways when the Dallas Stars won the Stanley Cup on one goal, even though Dallas forward Brett Hull's skate was clearly in the crease. The goal was allowed to stand, and the league changed the rule the following year to allow the referee to use his judgment in disallowing a goal.

That's Two Minutes for Diving

A disturbing trend has found its way into hockey. A phenomenon seen mostly in the sport of soccer, diving has unfortunately become a tool for some players to give their team a two-minute power play advantage. Players began falling all over the ice—so much so that the league instituted a new minor penalty for the start of the 2005–06 season. The new rule penalizes players for any obvious attempts to draw a penalty by diving, embellishing a fall or reaction or feigning an injury.

A prime example of why this rule was instated came during a playoff game between the Boston Bruins and the Montréal Canadiens. When Canadiens forward Mike Ribeiro was hit at centre ice, he immediately fell to the ice in what appeared to be extreme pain. Yet just a few moments later, he could be seen on the bench taunting the Bruins players and was soon back out on the ice skating in fine form—a move you would expect to see from a soccer player and not in the game of hockey. But as always, the league is constantly changing.

A New Twist on the Delay of Game Rule

Among the plethora of new NHL rules to hit the league in the 2005–06 season, the league added a rule that has been a pain in the neck for all defencemen and coaches across the league.

The new rule states that if any player in his defensive zone shoots the puck directly (not deflected) out of the playing area, a two-minute minor penalty will automatically be assessed. If the puck is shot into the players' bench, a penalty will not be assessed.

The league rule was created to discourage defencemen from shooting the puck out of their zone when the other team is on the attack. But for the league's defencemen, whose job it is to relieve offensive pressure, it has become an increasingly annoying penalty. Previously, a penalty was given when it was deemed that the defenceman intentionally shot the puck into the stands, but now, no matter the circumstance, a penalty is called if the puck leaves the playing surface. Many times during the year, defencemen, forwards and even goaltenders have been assessed penalties when it clearly wasn't their intention to delay the game. But the rule is clear, and many goals have been scored on power plays because of the new rule, leaving frustrated players and angry coaches.

The End of the Wandering Goaltender

Another new rule change to increase offense for the 2005–06 season has been to limit the area where goaltenders can play the puck by making it a penalty if the goalie wanders into the restricted area in the corners behind the icing line. Before the new rule, goaltenders were allowed to wander anywhere they wanted behind their own blue line. The league wanted to eliminate goalies coming out of their nets to play the puck on dump-ins, hoping to encourage more turnovers and therefore more offence.

The new rule has worked well enough to deter goaltenders from playing the puck in the corners, but now many goaltenders try to get to the puck before it crosses the line and only a few goaltenders have been penalized for wandering into the forbidden zone.

The End of the Incredible Expanding Goaltenders

Anyone who watched hockey prior to about 1995 must surely have noticed that goaltenders across the league seemed to be growing in size. This was not because general managers were recruiting larger players, but because many goaltenders were wearing equipment that belied their tiny frames underneath.

Not that he is the only culprit, but Anaheim Mighty Ducks goaltender Jean Sebastien Giguere looked rather large in nets before the new rules were instated. The main area of complaint against most goalies was the extremely large catching and blocking gloves and the size of the goaltenders' leg pads. The official NHL rulebook contains all the new dimensions netminders must follow when it comes to their equipment. One day, some eccentric general manager might come along and hire a large sumo wrestler to sit in the net and cover all angles without violating the equipment rules, but for now, the goalies are back to normal size.

The Shootout

In another effort to please the viewing public and win more fans back into the fold of professional hockey consumption, the National Hockey League brain trust has instituted its best attraction yet—the shootout.

During the regular season only, if both teams fail to break a tie after a five-minute overtime period, they will enter into a shootout. This is where it gets exciting. The coaches select three players, each one getting a breakaway shot on the goaltender until the tie is broken. Fans seem to love the new format because it brings a sense of anticipation when either team can win the game with just one shot. Whether it's here to stay is another story.

Chapter Eleven
TRADES, DEFECTIONS, DRAFTS AND SURPRISE MOVES

Infamous Trades, Defections, Drafts and Surprise Moves

Detroit Trades Red Kelley to Toronto

The Norris Trophy–winning defenceman Red Kelley helped the Detroit Red Wings to four Stanley Cups in the early '50s. But when Kelley was quoted in a magazine saying that Red Wings boss Jack Adams once made him play in a game despite having a cracked bone, he was promptly traded to Toronto for defenceman Marc Reaume. Jack Adams was known for his temper and lack of patience with anyone who disagreed with him, so even though Kelly was an all-star defenceman, Adams traded him. Red Kelley went on to help the Toronto Maple Leafs to four Stanley Cups in the '60s, while Reaume played only 47 games as a Red Wing.

Phil Esposito Goes to Boston

Boston's loss of Ken Dryden in the draft was quickly rectified by the acquisition of Phil Esposito from the Chicago Blackhawks. Esposito and the

Chicago management had never seen eye to eye. Esposito approached the game less seriously than the men in suits liked, and the conflict eventually came to the boiling point at the end of the 1966–67 regular season. When the Blackhawks were celebrating their first-ever first-place finish, Esposito, obviously drunk on champagne, approached general manager Tommy Ivan. Esposito told him that they could win the Cup if Ivan didn't screw up the chemistry on the team. When Chicago lost in the semifinals to Toronto, Esposito was traded to Boston for the start of the next season. Esposito and the Bruins went on to break many scoring records and win two Stanley Cup championships, while Chicago's fortunes waxed and waned over the next decade.

The Trade Heard around the World

The Oilers had just come off another Stanley Cup victory in 1988 when rumours of a big trade involving one of the Oilers began to circulate through the hockey world. When Oilers management called a press conference on August 8, 1988, people finally realized their fears were about to come true. The room fell silent as Pocklington uttered the words that all of Canada did not want to hear.

"Gretzky has been traded to the Los Angeles Kings," he said, as flashes from the news photographers' cameras illuminated the room.

Pocklington announced that Gretzky had been packaged along with Marty McSorley and Mike Krushelnyski in return for Jimmy Carson and Martin Gelinas, along with several draft picks and $15 million. After Pocklington finished announcing the business of the trade, Gretzky approached the microphone with a sad look on his face.

"For the benefit of Wayne Gretzky, my new wife and our expected child in the new year, it would be for the benefit of everyone involved to let me play for the Los Angeles Kings," said Gretzky, pausing to take a deep breath. "I promised Mess [Mark Messier] I wouldn't do this," he said, wiping the tears from his eyes.

The hockey world was in collective shock. The boy from Brantford, Ontario, who grew up before their eyes into the greatest hockey player in the game, had been traded. To make matters worse, it was to an American team.

Although he never won another Cup, just his presence on the Los Angeles Kings squad brought fresh attention to hockey in the United States at a time when it needed his star power.

The Infamous Patrick Roy Trade

Every Canadiens fan remembers that game on December 5, 1995, against the Detroit Red Wings at the Montréal Forum when Habs coach Mario Tremblay refused to take Roy out of the net after he let in 9 goals. Embarrassed by the ordeal and the fact that Roy and Tremblay had never seen eye-to-eye, Roy took off his helmet and walked past Tremblay on the bench. Roy told Canadiens president Ronald Corey that he had played his last game as a Montréal Canadien. A few days later, Roy was traded along with Mike Keane to the Colorado Avalanche for Jocelyn Thibault, Andrei Kovalenko and Martin Ruchinsky. The next season, Roy won the Stanley Cup with the Avalanche and took home the Conn Smythe Trophy as the playoff's most valuable player. The Canadiens have not been the same since his departure.

Joe Thornton Goes to San Jose

The Boston Bruins management team smacked their collective heads when they looked at the amazing season their team's former captain had with the San Jose Sharks. Wanting to change the team's losing ways, Bruins general manager Mike O'Connell decided to trade their captain, Joe Thornton, mid-season for a few good young Sharks—forwards Wayne Primeau and Marco Sturm and defenceman Brad Stuart.

Even with the new additions to the team, the Bruins still continued their losing ways and failed to make the playoffs. Joe Thornton, on the other hand, had a great season with the Sharks, scoring over 100 points and helping his team into the 2006 playoffs. At the end of the 2006 regular season, Bruins management still had their jobs.

Dany Heatley for Marion Hossa— Straight Up

Although having either Dany Heatley or Marion Hossa on your team would improve your chances of winning the Stanley Cup, the Ottawa Senators and the Atlanta Thrashers thought they should trade players to see which could get them the closest to the championship.

The Ottawa Senators came out of the trade looking the smartest. Dany Heatley has found a comfortable spot on the Senators' top line and took Ottawa far into the 2006 playoffs.

Hossa had a good year with the Atlanta Thrashers, but the team sat just out of reach of a playoff spot, failing to make the battle for the Cup by a couple of points.

Draft Blunders
1980: Canadiens select first overall

For the first time since 1971, when they chose Guy Lafleur, the Montréal Canadiens had the first choice in the 1980 entry draft. They chose Doug Wickenheiser, who had played 556 games in Regina and scored 111 goals. Other players of note that the Canadiens passed on were Denis Savard, selected third overall by the Chicago Blackhawks;

Paul Coffey, selected sixth overall by Edmonton; and Jari Kurri, selected 69th overall, also by Edmonton.

1964: Boston Bruins select Ken Dryden 14th overall in the entry draft

Bruin fans are still slapping their heads over this one. When the Boston Bruins selected Ken Dryden, they were getting a proven goaltender who was a star in the minors and was poised to become one of the best in the league. The Bruins decided to trade his rights to the Montréal Canadiens along with Alex Campbell for Guy Allen and Paul Reid. Neither Allen nor Reid played one minute in the National Hockey League, whereas Ken Dryden led the Canadiens to six Stanley Cups and secured a place in the Hockey Hall of Fame in 1983.

1970: The Canadiens trade for first round draft pick

The Montréal Canadiens made the deal of the decade when they traded Ernie Hicke and their first-round pick for the 1970 draft in exchange for the California Seals defenceman Francois Lacombe and that team's 1971 first-round pick. The Canadiens used that first-round draft pick to select Guy Lafleur. Lafleur helped the Canadiens dominate the '70s and won five Stanley Cups during his career.

1991: The Québec Nordiques draft
Eric Lindros

When Eric Lindros was made available for selection in the 1991 NHL entry draft, it was obvious that the Québec Nordiques were going to pick the high-scoring forward as their number-one choice. When they did choose Lindros, he refused to go to the team, not wanting to go to a small market like Québec. After months of legal proceedings, the Nordiques finally gave up trying to sign the whiny forward and traded his rights to the Philadelphia Flyers. Lindros should have stayed with the Nordiques, who won the Stanley Cup in 1996 (as the Colorado Avalanche). Lindros has yet to win the Cup and currently plays for the Toronto Maple Leafs.

Dark Horse Draft Picks

Luc Robitaille, selected 171st overall by the Los Angeles Kings at the 1984 entry draft. Robitaille has played 1384 games, scored 658 goals and made 720 assists so far. Not a bad deal for 171st overall.

Pavel Bure, selected 113th overall by the Vancouver Canucks at the 1989 entry draft. Bure scored 437 goals in 702 games. Nicknamed the "Russian Rocket" because he was so fast on the ice, his career ended early because of chronic injuries.

Pavol Demitra, selected 227th overall by the Ottawa Senators at the 1993 entry draft. Demitra has scored 230 goals so far in his career and is a constant threat when he is on the ice.

Brett Hull, selected 117th overall by the Calgary Flames at the 1984 entry draft. Hull has far surpassed the shadow of his father Bobby, quickly establishing himself as one of the best pure scorers in the league. He has scored 741 goals and 650 assists for a total of 1391 points.

Dominik Hasek, selected 207th overall by the Chicago Blackhawks in the 1983 entry draft. Hasek has gone on to have an outstanding career earning gold at the 1998 Winter Olympics and finally winning the Stanley Cup with the Detroit Red Wings in 2002.

Daniel Alfredsson, selected by the Ottawa Senators 133rd overall in the 1994 entry draft. The speedy captain of the Senators is a constant threat on the ice and a valuable asset to the franchise. He won the Rookie of the Year award in 1996 and has scored 240 goals in 654 games since he started in the NHL.

Doug Gilmour, selected 134th overall by the St. Louis Blues in the 1982 draft. Gilmour has had a remarkable career with every team he has played for and was one of the major reasons the Calgary Flames took home the Stanley Cup in 1989. He played 1474 games in the NHL, scoring 450 goals and 964 assists.

Andy Moog, selected 132nd overall by the Edmonton Oilers in the 1980 entry draft. Moog had a steady career with every team he played for, winning three Stanley Cups with the Edmonton Oilers.

Steve Larmer, selected 120th overall by the Chicago Blackhawks in the 1980 entry draft. A solid right winger, Larmer scored 441 goals and 571 assists in his 15 seasons in the NHL. He finally won the Stanley Cup as a member of the New York Rangers in 1994.

Rick Tocchet, selected 125th overall by the Philadelphia Flyers in the 1983 entry draft. An excellent defensive forward, Tocchet also could score goals when called upon, finishing his career with 440 goals and 512 assists for 952 points.

Theoren Fleury, selected 166th overall by the Calgary Flames in the 1987 draft. Despite the ups and downs in his career, Fleury has been an asset to every team he's played with, winning the Stanley Cup in his rookie year with the Calgary Flames. He retired having played 1084 games with 455 goals and 633 assists for a total of 1088 points.

Peter Bondra, selected 156th overall by the Washington Capitals in the 1990 entry draft. Since breaking into the league, Bondra hasn't scored less than 20 goals per season since his rookie year and has broken the 50-goal barrier once. In 1011 games, he has scored 490 goals and 377 assists.

Dino Ciccarelli, who wasn't even selected in the draft because he broke his leg as a junior. He was later signed to the Minnesota North Stars and ended up scoring 608 goals in his career in the National Hockey League.

Patrick Roy, selected 51st overall by the Montréal Canadiens in the 1984 entry draft. The reason he wasn't drafted earlier was his poor record in the minor leagues, but the Canadiens management saw something in the young Roy and signed him to the club. He would lead the Canadiens twice to the Stanley Cup before falling out with management in 1995.

Pavel Datsyuk, selected 171st overall in the 1998 NHL entry draft by the Detroit Red Wings. He has more than shown that he is a capable player in the NHL by scoring some of the nicest goals in the game today. With his creative skills on the ice, the Red Wings have a great player for years to come.

Top Draft Pick Failures

Claude Gauthier was selected first overall in the 1964 entry draft by the Detroit Red Wings but never played a game in the NHL, along with the other top four picks that year.

Rick Pagnutti was selected first overall in the 1967 expansion draft but never played a minute in the National Hockey League.

Andre Veilleux was selected first overall in the 1965 entry draft by the New York Rangers. New York Rangers had hoped Veilleux would make the team, but he never played a game in the NHL.

Ray Martymiuk was selected fifth overall by the Montréal Canadiens in the 1970 entry draft. The Canadiens passed on such notable players as Darryl Sittler and Mike Murphy for a goaltender who never played a game in the NHL.

Cam Connor was selected fifth overall by the Montréal Canadiens in the 1974 entry draft and only played 89 games, scoring 9 goals. The Canadiens missed such notable players as Bryan Trottier (22nd overall) and Tiger Williams (31st overall).

Daniel Tkaczuk was selected sixth overall by the Calgary Flames in the 1997 entry draft. Tkaczuk played only 19 games and scored 4 goals. Calgary passed on players such as Sergei Samsonov and Marian Hossa.

Scott Scissons was selected sixth overall by the New York Islanders in the 1990 entry draft. He played only two games in the NHL before being sent back to the minors. The Islanders passed on such wonderful draft opportunities as Derian Hatcher, Keith Tkachuk and Martin Brodeur.

Bjorn Johansson was selected fifth overall by the California Seals in the 1976 entry draft. He played only 15 games, scoring one goal and one assist. He was the first European player to be selected in the first round of the draft.

Rocky Trottier was selected eighth overall by the New Jersey Devils in the 1982 entry draft. He played only 38 games, scoring 6 goals and 4 assists before being sent back to the minors. Since he was the brother of Bryan Trottier, the Devils had hoped that the talent in the family was passed on. They were wrong.

Greg Vaydik was selected seventh overall by the Chicago Blackhawks in the 1975 entry draft. The Hawks were hoping to get a tough centre who could score goals as well as intimidate opponents, but Vaydik only played five games before being sent down to the minors.

Chapter Twelve

THE GREAT HOCKEY QUIZ

The Great Hockey Quiz

1. *Who is the only retired player in NHL history to have won the regular-season scoring title who has not been named to the Hockey Hall of Fame?*

    A. Roy Conacher   B. Max Bentley

    C. Busher Jackson   D. Herb Cain

2. *Who was the last Montréal Canadien to make it into the top 20 of the regular-season scoring leaders?*

    A. Mark Recchi   B. Pierre Turgeon

    C. Michael Ryder   D. Saku Koivu

3. *Which goaltender posted the first shutout in the National Hockey League?*

    A. Clint Benedict   B. Georges Vezina

    C. Hap Holmes   D. Bert Lindsay

4. *Who was the last goaltender in the NHL to play without a mask?*

    A. Wayne Stevenson   B. Andy Brown

    C. Gary Smith   D. Glenn Hall

5. *Which goaltender has the longest shutout streak in NHL history?*

   A. Terry Sawchuk   B. Brian Boucher

   C. Alex Connell   D. Bill Durnan

6. *Who wrote the theme song to the CBC's "Hockey Night in Canada"?*

   A. Singer-songwriter   B. Country legend
      Paul Anka   Stompin' Tom Connors

   C. '80s rocker Gowan   D. Composer Dolores
                                        Claman

7. *Who holds the record for the longest time without missing a game?*

   A. Gary Unger   B. Doug Jarvis

   C. Mike Gartner   D. Ray Bourque

8. *Which team currently holds the record for going the longest without winning the Stanley Cup?*

   A. Toronto Maple Leafs   B. Chicago Blackhawks

   C. St. Louis Blues   D. Los Angeles Kings

9. *Who is the only coach in NHL history to lose in 12 Stanley Cup finals?*

   A. Jack Adams   B. Scotty Bowman

   C. Dick Irvin   D. Punch Imlach

10. *Which former NHL tough guy fought an exhibition match against heavyweight champion Muhammad Ali?*

   A. Tiger Williams   B. Dave Semenko

   C. Dave Schultz   D. Paul Stewart

11. *Who holds the record for most points scored by a goaltender in one game?*

   A. Ron Hextall   B. Martin Brodeur

   C. Jeff Reese   D. Billy Smith

12. *What team scored the most total goals in an NHL season with a minimum of 70 games?*

A. The 1981–82
   Edmonton Oilers

B. The 1986–87
   Edmonton Oilers

C. The 1976–77
   Montréal Canadiens

D. The 1983–84
   Edmonton Oilers

13. *What is the highest number of empty-net goals scored by a team in one game?*

A. 1

B. 2

C. 4

D. 5

14. *Who signed the first multi-year million-dollar contract in professional hockey?*

A. Bobby Hull

B. Bobby Orr

C. Phil Esposito

D. Wayne Gretzky

15. *Which was the first NHL team to put players' names on the backs of the jerseys?*

A. Boston Bruins

B. Toronto Maple Leafs

C. New York Americans

D. Philadelphia Quakers

16. *In what year of the NHL did a player score the first goal on a penalty shot?*

A. 1934

B. 1922

C. 1930

D. 1918

17. *True or False:* There has never been an NHL game without a penalty being called?

18. *In what year was a hockey game first broadcast on television?*

A. 1940

B. 1936

C. 1952

D. 1938

19. *Which goaltender invented the trapper?*

    A. Turk Broda   B. Emile Francis

    C. Clint Benedict   D. Jacques Plante

20. *Which trophy did Jean Beliveau win first in 1965?*

    A. Conn Smythe Trophy   B. Bill Masterton Trophy

    C. Pearson Trophy   D. Lady Byng Trophy

Answers

1: *D.* Despite being a member of the Boston Bruins during their terrible 1943–44 season, **Herb Cain** was able to establish a record-breaking performance as the first player in the National Hockey League to break through the 80-point barrier. He remains the only retired player to have won the scoring title and not have a place in the Hockey Hall of Fame.

2: *A.* Not since the 1997–98 season, when **Mark Recchi** scored 72 points, have the Montréal Canadiens had a player who has cracked the top 20 in regular-season scoring.

3: *B.* On February 18, 1918, **Georges Vezina** of the Montréal Canadiens recorded the first shutout victory in NHL history when he blanked the Toronto Arenas 9–0. The shutout came in the third month of the NHL's first season.

4: *D.* Although he only played 62 games in the NHL, the Pittsburgh Penguins goaltender **Andy Brown** can say that he was the last goaltender ever to play without a face mask.

5: *C.* While Brian Boucher holds the modern-day record for five consecutive games without a goal (modern day is designated as everything after the 1943–44 season), **Alex Connell** of the 1927–28 Ottawa Senators recorded his sixth consecutive shutout on February 18, 1928, against the Montréal Canadiens in a 1–0 victory.

6: *D*. Canada's hockey anthem was penned by composer **Dolores Claman** and first broadcast across the country in 1967. The CBC's executives wanted a similar theme to American action shows like the "Mod Squad" to start millions of Canadians' Saturday night ritual.

7: *B*. Doug Jarvis played with three teams during the 12 years it took him to play 964 games, and he never missed one. The second-longest game streak was set by Gary Unger at 915 games. That record would be almost impossible today, with players getting injured all the time and the closer attention paid to things like concussions. During game number 761, Jarvis received a concussion after taking a hit from Randy Ladouceur. After a short stay in hospital overnight, he rejoined his team the next day for game number 762.

8: *B*. The **Chicago Blackhawks** have the dubious honour of being the team that has currently gone the longest without winning the Stanley Cup, last winning hockey's greatest prize in 1961, 44 years ago. The Toronto Maple Leafs have not won the Cup in 38 years, last winning in 1967. Both Los Angeles and St. Louis have never won the Cup in their 37 years of existence. The longest streak without winning the Cup is actually held by the New York Rangers, who finally won in 1994 after a drought of 54 years.

9: *C*. Although he won four Stanley Cups over his 28-year coaching career, **Dick Irvin** was not very lucky when it came to the Stanley Cup finals, losing 12 times. In his last year with the Canadiens, he lost to the Detroit Red Wings in the seventh game.

10: *B*. In the '80s, **Dave Semenko** fought a three-round exhibition match in Edmonton against Ali. Semenko trained really hard for the fight but was told to take it easy during the match by one of Ali's trainers. Neither man was seriously hurt during the fight.

11: *C*. While Ron Hextall and Martin Brodeur actually scored a goal, it was **Jeff Reese** of the Hartford Whalers who got 3 assists in one game on February 10, 1993.

12: *D*. The 1983–84 Edmonton Oilers were scoring machines. With players such as Gretzky, Messier, Coffey, Kurri and Anderson, the Edmonton Oilers scored 446 goals. The second-highest total is, of course, the Edmonton Oilers during the 1985–86 season, with 426 goals.

13: *D*. On April 5, 1970, the Montréal Canadiens faced the Chicago Blackhawks in the final game of the season. The New York Rangers were tied with the Canadiens for the final playoff spot but had the advantage in goals scored. The Canadiens needed to either win the game or score a large number of goals, but the Blackhawks were winning the game 5–2 in the third period and hope seemed to be fading for the Canadiens' chance at the playoffs. With only 10 minutes remaining in the period, Montréal coach Claude Ruel pulled goaltender Rogie Vachon in a last-ditch attempt to win the game. The Habs could not get around Hawks' goaltender Tony Esposito, and Chicago filled the Canadiens empty net with **5** goals.

14: *B*. Bobby Orr became hockey's first millionaire when he signed a five-year million-dollar contract with the Boston Bruins in 1971. Bobby Hull became the second millionaire when he signed a multi-year contract with the WHA's Winnipeg Jets.

15: *C*. In 1926, the **New York Americans** first put names on the backs of the players' jerseys in an attempt to market the team to the inexperienced fans in the United States. The National Hockey League did not make it mandatory for all players to wear their names on their uniforms until the 1970s.

16: *A*. Armand Mondu of the Montréal Canadiens took the first-ever penalty shot but did not score. It was Ralph 'Scotty' Bowman of the St. Louis Eagles who scored on the New York Americans on November 13, **1934**.

17: *False*. On February 20, 1944, the Toronto Maple Leafs played an away game against the Chicago Blackhawks. Not only was the score at the end of the overtime period 0–0, but not one penalty was called during the most civil game of hockey ever played in the NHL.

18: *D*. The first NHL hockey game to be broadcast on TV took place on February 25, 1940, between the New York Rangers and the Montréal Canadiens, and it was seen by just over 300 people in a small area. But that was not the first live broadcast of a game. The first broadcast took place in England on October 29, **1938,** in a game between the Harringay Racers and Streatham for the British National Tournament transmitted by BBC Studios. The CBC's first hockey broadcast was in 1952 with the Montréal Canadiens and the Detroit Red Wings.

19: *B.* Prior to the invention of the trapper, goaltenders used gloves identical to those of the players. The Chicago Blackhawk's **Emile Francis** changed the position forever when he modified a first baseman's mitt in the 1947–48 season. After some initial protests, league president Clarence Campbell eventually approved it. Francis is also credited with the invention of the blocker, when he taped a layer of sponge rubber to his stick-side glove.

20: *A.* The **Conn Smythe Trophy** was first awarded to Jean Beliveau for his outstanding performance during the 1965 playoffs, scoring 8 goals and 8 assists and leading the Canadiens to the Stanley Cup.

Chapter Thirteen

Winners of Hockey's Hardware

Stanley Cup Winners since 1893

Year	Winner	W–L	Coach	Opponent
2006	Carolina Hurricanes	4–3	Peter Laviolette	Edmonton Oilers
2005	Stanley Cup not awarded because of labor disagreement lockout			
2004	Tampa Bay Lightning	4–3	John Tortorella	Calgary Flames
2003	New Jersey Devils	4–3	Pat Burns	Anaheim Mighty Ducks
2002	Detroit Red Wings	4–1	Scotty Bowman	Carolina Hurricanes
2001	Colorado Avalanche	4–3	Bob Hartley	New Jersey Devils
2000	New Jersey Devils	4–1	Larry Robinson	Dallas Stars
1999	Dallas Stars	4–2	Ken Hitchcock	Buffalo Sabres
1998	Detroit Red Wings	4–0	Scotty Bowman	Washington Capitals
1997	Detroit Red Wings	4–0	Scotty Bowman	Philadelphia Flyers
1996	Colorado Avalanche	4–0	Marc Crawford	Florida Panthers
1995	New Jersey Devils	4–0	Jacques Lemaire	Detroit Red Wings
1994	NY Rangers	4–3	Mike Keenan	Vancouver Canucks
1993	Montréal Canadiens	4–1	Jacques Demers	Los Angeles Kings
1992	Pittsburgh Penguins	4–0	Scotty Bowman	Chicago Blackhawks
1991	Pittsburgh Penguins	4–2	Bob Johnson	Minnesota North Stars
1990	Edmonton Oilers	4–1	John Muckler	Boston Bruins
1989	Calgary Flames	4–2	Terry Crisp	Montréal Canadiens

Stanley Cup Continued

Year	Winner	W–L	Coach	Opponent
1988	Edmonton Oilers	4–0	Glen Sather	Boston Bruins
1987	Edmonton Oilers	4–3	Glen Sather	Philadelphia Flyers
1986	Montréal Canadiens	4–1	Jean Perron	Calgary Flames
1985	Edmonton Oilers	4–1	Glen Sather	Philadelphia Flyers
1984	Edmonton Oilers	4–1	Glen Sather	NY Islanders
1983	NY Islanders	4–0	Al Arbour	Edmonton Oilers
1982	NY Islanders	4–0	Al Arbour	Vancouver Canucks
1981	NY Islanders	4–1	Al Arbour	Minnesota North Stars
1980	NY Islanders	4–2	Al Arbour	Philadelphia Flyers
1979	Montréal Canadiens	4–1	Scotty Bowman	NY Rangers
1978	Montréal Canadiens	4–2	Scotty Bowman	Boston Bruins
1977	Montréal Canadiens	4–0	Scotty Bowman	Boston Bruins
1976	Montréal Canadiens	4–0	Scotty Bowman	Philadelphia Flyers
1975	Philadelphia Flyers	4–2	Fred Shero	Buffalo Sabres
1974	Philadelphia Flyers	4–2	Fred Shero	Boston Bruins
1973	Montréal Canadiens	4–2	Scotty Bowman	Chicago Blackhawks
1972	Boston Bruins	4–2	Tom Johnson	NY Rangers
1971	Montréal Canadiens	4–3	Al MacNeil	Chicago Blackhawks
1970	Boston Bruins	4–0	Harry Sinden	St. Louis Blues
1969	Montréal Canadiens	4–0	Claude Ruel	St. Louis Blues
1968	Montréal Canadiens	4–0	Toe Blake	St. Louis Blues
1967	Toronto Maple Leafs	4–2	Punch Imlach	Montréal Canadiens
1966	Montréal Canadiens	4–2	Toe Blake	Detroit Red Wings
1965	Montréal Canadiens	4–3	Toe Blake	Chicago Blackhawks
1964	Toronto Maple Leafs	4–3	Punch Imlach	Detroit Red Wings
1963	Toronto Maple Leafs	4–1	Punch Imlach	Detroit Red Wings
1962	Toronto Maple Leafs	4–2	Punch Imlach	Chicago Blackhawks
1961	Chicago Blackhawks	4–2	Rudy Pilous	Detroit Red Wings
1960	Montréal Canadiens	4–3	Toe Blake	Toronto Maple Leafs
1959	Montréal Canadiens	4–1	Toe Blake	Toronto Maple Leafs
1958	Montréal Canadiens	4–2	Toe Blake	Boston Bruins

Stanley Cup Continued

Year	Winner	W–L	Coach	Opponent
1957	Montréal Canadiens	4–1	Toe Blake	Boston Bruins
1956	Montréal Canadiens	4–1	Toe Blake	Detroit Red Wings
1955	Detroit Red Wings	4–3	Jimmy Skiner	Montréal Canadiens
1954	Detroit Red Wings	4–3	Tommy Ivan	Montréal Canadiens
1953	Montréal Canadiens	4–1	Dick Irvin	Boston Bruins
1952	Detroit Red Wings	4–0	Tommy Ivan	Montréal Canadiens
1951	Toronto Maple Leafs	4–1	Joe Primeau	Montréal Canadiens
1950	Detroit Red Wings	4–3	Tommy Ivan	NY Rangers
1949	Toronto Maple Leafs	4–0	Hap Day	Detroit Red Wings
1948	Toronto Maple Leafs	4–0	Hap Day	Detroit Red Wings
1947	Toronto Maple Leafs	4–2	Hap Day	Montréal Canadiens
1946	Montréal Canadiens	4–1	Dick Irvin	Boston Bruins
1945	Toronto Maple Leafs	4–3	Hap Day	Detroit Red Wings
1944	Montréal Canadiens	4–0	Dick Irvin	Chicago Blackhawks
1943	Detroit Red Wings	4–0	Jack Adams	Boston Bruins
1942	Toronto Maple Leafs	4–3	Hap Day	Detroit Red Wings
1941	Boston Bruins	4–0	Cooney Weiland	Detroit Red Wings
1940	NY Rangers	4–2	Frank Boucher	Toronto Maple Leafs
1939	Boston Bruins	4–1	Art Ross	Toronto Maple Leafs
1938	Chicago Blackhawks	3–1	Bill Stewart	Toronto Maple Leafs
1937	Detroit Red Wings	3–2	Jack Adams	NY Rangers
1936	Detroit Red Wings	3–1	Jack Adams	Toronto Maple Leafs
1935	Montréal Maroons	3–0	Tommy Gorman	Toronto Maple Leafs
1934	Chicago Blackhawks	3–1	Tommy Gorman	Detroit Red Wings
1933	NY Rangers	3–1	Lester Patrick	Toronto Maple Leafs
1932	Toronto Maple Leafs	3–0	Dick Irvin	NY Rangers
1931	Montréal Canadiens	3–2	Cecil Hart	Chicago Blackhawks
1930	Montréal Canadiens	2–0	Cecil Hart	Boston Bruins
1929	Boston Bruins	2–0	Cy Denneny	NY Rangers
1928	NY Rangers	3–2	Lester Patrick	Montréal Maroons
1927	Ottawa Senators	2–0	Dave Gill	Boston Bruins

Stanley Cup Continued

Year	Winner	W–L	Coach	Opponent
1926	Montréal Maroons	3–1	Eddie Gerard	Victoria Cougars
1925	Victoria Cougars	3–1	Lester Patrick	Montréal Canadiens
1924	Montréal Canadiens	2–0	Leo Dandurand	Calgary Tigers
		2–0		Vancouver Maroons
1923	Ottawa Senators	2–0	Pete Green	Edmonton Eskimos
		3–1		Vancouver Maroons
1922	Toronto St. Patricks	3–2	Eddie Powers	Vancouver Millionaires
1921	Ottawa Senators	3–2	Pete Green	Vancouver Millionaires
1920	Ottawa Senators	3–2	Pete Green	Seattle Metropolitans
1919	Series between Montréal and Seattle cancelled after influenza epidemic			
1918	Toronto Arenas	3–2	Dick Carroll	Vancouver Millionaires

Stanley Cup Winners
Prior to Formation of NHL in 1917

Season	Champion	Coach (or *Captain)
1916–17	Seattle Metropolitans	Pete Muldoon
1915–16	Montréal Canadiens	George Kennedy
1914–15	Vancouver Millionaires	Frank Patrick
1913–14	Toronto Blueshirts	Scotty Davidson*
1912–13	Quebec Bulldogs	Joe Malone*
1911–12	Quebec Bulldogs	C. Nolan
1910–11	Ottawa Senators	Bruce Stuart*
1909–10	Montréal Wanderers	Pud Glass*
1908–09	Ottawa Senators	Bruce Stuart*
1907–08	Montréal Wanderers	Cecil Blachford
1906–07	Montréal Wanderers	Cecil Blachford
1905–06	Kenora Thistles	Tommy Phillips*
1904–05	Montréal Wanderers	Cecil Blachford*
1903–04	Ottawa Silver Seven	A.T. Smith
1902–03	Ottawa Silver Seven	A.T. Smith
1901–02	Ottawa Silver Seven	A.T. Smith
1900–01	Montréal AAA	C. McKerrow
1899–00	Winnipeg Victorias	D.H. Bain
1900–01	Montréal Shamrocks	H.J. Trihey*
1899–00	Montréal Shamrocks	H.J. Trihey*
1898–99	Montréal Victorias	F. Richardson
1897–98	Montréal Victorias	Mike Grant*
1896–97	Montréal Victorias	Mike Grant*
1895–96	Winnipeg Victorias	J.C.G. Armytage
1894–95	Montréal Victorias	Mike Grant*
1893–94	Montréal AAA	
1892–93	Montréal AAA	

Hart Memorial Trophy: Awarded to the Regular Season's Most Valuable Player

The Hart Trophy was the NHL's first individual trophy, donated by Dr. David Hart, father of Cecil Hart who was the former coach and manager of the Montréal Canadiens. In 1960, the original trophy was retired to the Hockey Hall of Fame and the new one was renamed the Hart Memorial Trophy.

Year	Player	Team
2006	Joe Thornton	San Jose Sharks
2005	No Winner—Lockout	
2004	Martin St. Louis	Tampa Bay Lightning
2003	Peter Forsberg	Colorado Avalanche
2002	Jose Theodore	Montréal Canadiens
2001	Joe Sakic	Colorado Avalanche
2000	Chris Pronger	St. Louis Blues
1999	Jaromir Jagr	Pittsburgh Penguins
1998	Dominik Hasek	Buffalo Sabres
1997	Dominik Hasek	Buffalo Sabres
1996	Mario Lemieux	Pittsburgh Penguins
1995	Eric Lindros	Philadelphia Flyers
1994	Sergei Fedorov	Detroit Red Wings
1993	Mario Lemieux	Pittsburgh Penguins
1992	Mark Messier	New York Rangers
1991	Brett Hull	St. Louis Blues
1990	Mark Messier	Edmonton Oilers
1989	Wayne Gretzky	Edmonton Oilers
1988	Mario Lemieux	Pittsburgh Penguins
1987	Wayne Gretzky	Edmonton Oilers

Hart Memorial Continued

Year	Player	Team
1986	Wayne Gretzky	Edmonton Oilers
1985	Wayne Gretzky	Edmonton Oilers
1984	Wayne Gretzky	Edmonton Oilers
1983	Wayne Gretzky	Edmonton Oilers
1982	Wayne Gretzky	Edmonton Oilers
1981	Wayne Gretzky	Edmonton Oilers
1980	Wayne Gretzky	Edmonton Oilers
1979	Bryan Trottier	New York Islanders
1978	Guy Lafleur	Montréal Canadiens
1977	Guy Lafleur	Montréal Canadiens
1976	Bobby Clarke	Philadelphia Flyers
1975	Bobby Clarke	Philadelphia Flyers
1974	Phil Esposito	Boston Bruins
1973	Bobby Clarke	Philadelphia Flyers
1972	Bobby Orr	Boston Bruins
1971	Bobby Orr	Boston Bruins
1970	Bobby Orr	Boston Bruins
1969	Phil Esposito	Boston Bruins
1968	Stan Mikita	Chicago Blackhawks
1967	Stan Mikita	Chicago Blackhawks
1966	Bobby Hull	Chicago Blackhawks
1965	Bobby Hull	Chicago Blackhawks
1964	Jean Beliveau	Montréal Canadiens
1963	Gordie Howe	Detroit Red Wings
1962	Jacques Plante	Montréal Canadiens
1961	Bernie Geoffrion	Montréal Canadiens
1960	Gordie Howe	Detroit Red Wings
1959	Andy Bathgate	New York Rangers
1958	Gordie Howe	Detroit Red Wings
1957	Gordie Howe	Detroit Red Wings
1956	Ted Kennedy	Toronto Maple Leafs
1955	Al Rollins	Chicago Blackhawks

Hart Memorial Continued

Year	Player	Team
1954	Al Rollins	Chicago Blackhawks
1953	Gordie Howe	Detroit Red Wings
1952	Gordie Howe	Detroit Red Wings
1951	Milt Schmidt	Boston Bruins
1950	Chuck Rayne	New York Rangers
1949	Sid Abel	Detroit Red Wings
1948	Buddy O'Connor	New York Rangers
1947	Maurice Richard	Montréal Canadiens
1946	Max Bentley	Chicago Blackhawks
1945	Elmer Lach	Montréal Canadiens
1944	Babe Pratt	Toronto Maple Leafs
1943	Bill Cowley	Boston Bruins
1942	Tom Anderson	New York Americans
1941	Bill Cowley	Boston Bruins
1940	Ebbie Goodfellow	Detroit Red Wings
1939	Toe Blake	Montréal Canadiens
1938	Eddie Shore	Boston Bruins
1937	Babe Siebert	Montréal Canadiens
1936	Eddie Shore	Boston Bruins
1935	Eddie Shore	Boston Bruins
1934	Aurel Joliat	Montréal Canadiens
1933	Eddie Shore	Boston Bruins
1932	Howie Morenz	Montréal Canadiens
1931	Howie Morenz	Montréal Canadiens
1930	Nels Stewart	Montréal Maroons
1929	Roy Worters	N.Y. Americans
1928	Howie Morenz	Montréal Canadiens
1927	Herb Gardiner	Montréal Canadiens
1926	Nels Stewart	Montréal Maroons
1925	Billy Burch	Hamilton
1924	Frank Nighbor	Ottawa

Conn Smythe Trophy Winners: Awarded to the Most Valuable Player in the Playoffs

The Conn Smythe Trophy was named after Conn Smythe, who built the Hockey Hall of Fame and was the owner of the Toronto Maple Leafs. That is why the trophy depicts the old Maple Leaf Gardens.

Year	Player	Team
2006	Cam Ward	Carolina Hurricanes
2005	No Winner—Lockout	
2003	Jean-Sebastien Giguere	Anaheim Mighty Ducks
2002	Nicklas Lidstrom	Detroit Red Wings
2001	Patrick Roy	Colorado Avalanche
1999	Joe Nieuwendyk	Dallas Stars
1998	Steve Yzerman	Detroit Red Wings
1997	Mike Vernon	Detroit Red Wings
1996	Joe Sakic	Colorado Avalanche
1995	Claude Lemieux	New Jersey Devils
1994	Brian Leetch	New York Rangers
1993	Patrick Roy	Montréal Canadiens
1992	Mario Lemieux	Pittsburgh Penguins
1991	Mario Lemieux	Pittsburgh Penguins
1990	Bill Ranford	Edmonton Oilers
1989	Al MacInnis	Calgary Flames
1988	Wayne Gretzky	Edmonton Oilers
1987	Ron Hextall	Philadelphia Flyers
1986	Patrick Roy	Montréal Canadiens
1985	Wayne Gretzky	Edmonton Oilers
1984	Mark Messier	Edmonton Oilers
1983	Billy Smith	New York Islanders
1982	Mike Bossy	New York Islanders
1981	Butch Goring	New York Islanders

Conn Smythe Trophy Continued

Year	Player	Team
1980	Bryan Trottier	New York Islanders
1979	Bob Gainey	Montréal Canadiens
1978	Larry Robinson	Montréal Canadiens
1977	Guy Lafleur	Montréal Canadiens
1976	Reggie Leach	Philadelphia Flyers
1975	Bernie Parent	Philadelphia Flyers
1974	Bernie Parent	Philadelphia Flyers
1973	Yvan Cournoyer	Montréal Canadiens
1972	Bobby Orr	Boston Bruins
1971	Ken Dryden	Montréal Canadiens
1970	Bobby Orr	Boston Bruins
1969	Serge Savard	Montréal Canadiens
1968	Glenn Hall	St. Louis Blues
1967	Dave Keon	Edmonton Oilers
1966	Roger Crozier	Detroit Red Wings
1965	Jean Beliveau	Montréal Canadiens

Art Ross Memorial Trophy: Awarded to NHL Top Scorer (first awarded in 1948)

The Art Ross Trophy is awarded in honour of Art Ross, who played, refereed, coached and managed in his long professional hockey career. As a tough defenceman, he won two Stanley Cups, with the Kenora Thistles in 1907 and the Montréal Wanderers in 1908. He also coached the Boston Bruins to three Stanley Cup Championships.

Year	Player	Team
2006	Joe Thornton	San Jose Sharks
2005	No Winner—Lockout	
2004	Martin St-Louis	Tampa Bay Lightning
2003	Peter Forsberg	Colorado Avalanche
2002	Jarome Iginla	Calgary Flames
2001	Jaromir Jagr	Pittsburgh Penguins
2000	Jaromir Jagr	Pittsburgh Penguins
1999	Jaromir Jagr	Pittsburgh Penguins
1998	Jaromir Jagr	Pittsburgh Penguins
1997	Mario Lemieux	Pittsburgh Penguins
1996	Mario Lemieux	Pittsburgh Penguins
1995	Jaromir Jagr	Pittsburgh Penguins
1994	Wayne Gretzky	Los Angeles Kings
1993	Mario Lemieux	Pittsburgh Penguins
1992	Mario Lemieux	Pittsburgh Penguins
1991	Wayne Gretzky	Los Angeles Kings
1990	Wayne Gretzky	Los Angeles Kings
1989	Mario Lemieux	Pittsburgh Penguins
1988	Mario Lemieux	Pittsburgh Penguins
1987	Wayne Gretzky	Edmonton Oilers

Art Ross Memorial Continued

Year	Player	Team
1986	Wayne Gretzky	Edmonton Oilers
1985	Wayne Gretzky	Edmonton Oilers
1984	Wayne Gretzky	Edmonton Oilers
1983	Wayne Gretzky	Edmonton Oilers
1982	Wayne Gretzky	Edmonton Oilers
1981	Wayne Gretzky	Edmonton Oilers
1980	Marcel Dionne	Los Angeles Kings
1979	Bryan Trottier	New York Islanders
1978	Guy Lafleur	Montréal Canadiens
1977	Guy Lafleur	Montréal Canadiens
1976	Guy Lafleur	Montréal Canadiens
1975	Bobby Orr	Boston Bruins
1974	Phil Esposito	Boston Bruins
1973	Phil Esposito	Boston Bruins
1972	Phil Esposito	Boston Bruins
1971	Phil Esposito	Boston Bruins
1970	Bobby Orr	Boston Bruins
1969	Phil Esposito	Boston Bruins
1968	Stan Mikita	Chicago Blackhawks
1967	Stan Mikita	Chicago Blackhawks
1966	Bobby Hull	Chicago Blackhawks
1965	Stan Mikita	Chicago Blackhawks
1964	Stan Mikita	Chicago Blackhawks
1963	Stan Mikita	Chicago Blackhawks
1962	Bobby Hull	Chicago Blackhawks
1961	Bernie Geoffrion	Montréal Canadiens
1960	Bobby Hull	Chicago Blackhawks
1959	Dickie Moore	Montréal Canadiens
1958	Dickie Moore	Montréal Canadiens
1957	Gordie Howe	Detroit Red Wings
1956	Jean Beliveau	Montréal Canadiens

Art Ross Memorial Continued

Year	Player	Team
1955	Bernie Geoffrion	Montréal Canadiens
1954	Gordie Howe	Detroit Red Wings
1953	Gordie Howe	Detroit Red Wings
1952	Gordie Howe	Detroit Red Wings
1951	Gordie Howe	Detroit Red Wings
1950	Ted Lindsay	Detroit Red Wings
1949	Roy Conacher	Chicago Blackhawks
1948	Elmer Lach	Montréal Canadiens
1947	Max Bentley	Chicago Blackhawks
1946	Max Bentley	Chicago Blackhawks
1945	Elmer Lach	Montréal Canadiens
1944	Herb Cain	Boston Bruins
1943	Doug Bentley	Chicago Blackhawkss
1942	Bryan Hextall	New York Rangers
1941	Bill Cowley	Boston Bruins
1940	Milt Schmidt	Boston Bruins
1939	Toe Blake	Montréal Canadiens
1938	Gordie Drillon	Toronto Maple Leafs
1937	Sweeney Schriner	New York Americans
1936	Sweeney Schriner	New York Americans
1935	Charlie Conacher	Toronto Maple Leafs
1934	Charlie Conacher	Toronto Maple Leafs
1933	Bill Cook	New York Rangers
1932	Busher Jackson	Toronto Maple Leafs
1931	Howie Morenz	Montréal Canadiens
1930	Cooney Weiland	Boston Bruins
1929	Ace Bailey	Toronto Maple Leafs
1928	Howie Morenz	Montréal Canadiens
1927	Bill Cook	New York Rangers
1926	Nels Stewart	Montréal Maroons
1925	Babe Dye	Toronto St. Patricks

Art Ross Memorial Continued

Year	Player	Team
1924	Cy Denneny	Ottawa Senators
1923	Babe Dye	Toronto St. Patricks
1922	Punch Broadbent	Ottawa Senators
1921	Newsy Lalonde	Montréal Canadiens
1920	Joe Malone	Québec Bulldogs
1919	Newsy Lalonde	Montréal Canadiens
1918	Joe Malone	Montréal Canadiens

Vezina Trophy: Awarded to the Best Goaltender During the Regular Season

The Vezina Trophy is awarded in honour of former Montréal Canadiens goaltender Georges Vezina, whose playing career ended when he contracted tuberculosis and later died from the disease. The Montréal Canadiens donated the trophy after his death.

Year	Player	Team
2006	Mikka Kiprusoff	Calgary Flames
2005	No Winner—Lockout	
2004	Martin Brodeu	New Jersey Devils
2003	Martin Brodeu	New Jersey Devils
2002	José Théodore	Montréal Canadiens
2001	Dominik Hasek	Buffalo Sabres
2000	Olaf Kölzig	Washington Capitals
1999	Dominik Hasek	Buffalo Sabres
1998	Dominik Hasek	Buffalo Sabres
1997	Dominik Hasek	Buffalo Sabres
1996	Jim Carey	Washington Capitals
1995	Dominik Hasek	Buffalo Sabres
1994	Dominik Hasek	Buffalo Sabres
1993	Ed Belfour	Chicago Blackhawks
1992	Patrick Roy	Montréal Canadiens
1991	Ed Belfour	Chicago Blackhawks
1990	Patrick Roy	Montréal Canadiens
1989	Patrick Roy	Montréal Canadiens
1988	Grant Fuhr	Edmonton Oilers
1987	Ron Hextall	Philadelphia Flyers
1986	John Vanbiesbrouck	New York Rangers

Vezina Trophy Continued

Year	Player	Team
1985	Pelle Lindbergh	Philadelphia Flyers
1984	Tom Barrasso	Buffalo Sabres
1983	Pete Peeters	Boston Bruins
1982	Billy Smith	New York Islanders
1981	Denis Herron	Montréal Canadiens
	Michel Larocque	Montréal Canadiens
	Richard Sevigny	Montréal Canadiens
1980	Don Edwards	Buffalo Sabres
	Bob Sauve	Buffalo Sabres
1979	Ken Dryden	Montréal Canadiens
	Michel Larocqu	Montréal Canadiens
1978	Ken Dryden	Montréal Canadiens
	Michel Larocque	Montréal Canadiens
1977	Ken Dryden	Montréal Canadiens
	Michel Larocque	Montréal Canadiens
1976	Ken Dryden	Montréal Canadiens
1975	Bernie Parent	Philadelphia Flyers
1974	Tony Esposito	Chicago Blackhawks
	Bernie Parent	Philadelphia Flyers
1973	Ken Dryden	Montréal Canadiens
1972	Tony Esposito	Chicago Blackhawks
	Gary Smith	Chicago Blackhawks
1971	Eddie Giacomin	New York Rangers
	Gilles Villemure	New York Rangers
1970	Tony Esposito	Chicago Blackhawks
1969	Glenn Hall	St. Louis Blues
	Jacques Plante	St. Louis Blues
1968	Rogatien Vachon	Montréal Canadiens
	Gump Worsley	Montréal Canadiens
1967	Glenn Hall	Chicago Blackhawks
	Denis DeJordy	Chicago Blackhawks

Vezina Trophy Continued

Year	Player	Team
1966	Gump Worsley	Montréal Canadiens
	Charlie Hodge	Montréal Canadiens
1965	Johnny Bower	Toronto Maple Leafs
	Terry Sawchuk	Toronto Maple Leafs
1964	Charlie Hodge	Montréal Canadiens
1963	Glenn Hall	Chicago Blackhawks
1962	Jacques Plante	Montréal Canadiens
1961	Johnny Bower	Toronto Maple Leafs
1960	Jacques Plante	Montréal Canadiens
1959	Jacques Plante	Montréal Canadiens
1958	Jacques Plante	Montréal Canadiens
1957	Jacques Plante	Montréal Canadiens
1956	Jacques Plante	Montréal Canadiens
1955	Terry Sawchuk	Detroit Red Wings
1954	Harry Lumley	Toronto Maple Leafs
1953	Terry Sawchuk	Detroit Red Wings
1952	Terry Sawchuk	Detroit Red Wings
1951	Al Rollins	Toronto Maple Leafs
1950	Bill Durnan	Montréal Canadiens
1949	Bill Durnan	Montréal Canadiens
1948	Turk Broda	Toronto Maple Leafs
1947	Bill Durnan	Montréal Canadiens
1946	Bill Durnan	Montréal Canadiens
1945	Bill Durnan	Montréal Canadiens
1944	Bill Durnan	Montréal Canadiens
1943	Johnny Mowers	Detroit Red Wings
1942	Frank Brimsek	Boston Bruins
1941	Turk Broda	Toronto Maple Leafs
1940	David Kerr	New York Rangers
1939	Frank Brimsek	Boston Bruins
1938	Tiny Thompson	Boston Bruins

Vezina Trophy Continued

Year	Player	Team
1937	Normie Smith	Detroit Red Wings
1936	Tiny Thompson	Boston Bruins
1935	Lorne Chabot	Chicago Blackhawks
1934	Chuck Gardiner	Chicago Blackhawks
1933	Tiny Thompson	Boston Bruins
1932	Chuck Gardiner	Chicago Blackhawks
1931	Roy Worters	New York Americans
1930	Tiny Thompson	Boston Bruins
1929	George Hainsworth	Montréal Canadiens
1928	George Hainsworth	Montréal Canadiens
1927	George Hainsworth	Montréal Canadiens

Notes on Sources

Allen, Kevin, and Bob Duff. *Without Fear: Hockey's 50 Greatest Goaltenders*. Chicago: Triumph Books, 2002.

Conner, Floyd. *Hockey's Most Wanted*. Washington: Brassey's, Inc, 2002.

Diamond, Dan, ed. *Total NHL*. Toronto: Dan Diamond and Associates, 2003.

Diamond, Dan and Eric Zweig. *Hockey's Glory Days: The 1950s and '60s*. Kansas City: Andrews McMeel Publishing, 2003.

Dryden, Ken. *The Game*. Toronto: Wiley Press, 2005.

Dryden, Steve. *The Magic, the Legend, the Numbers: Total Gretzky*. Toronto: McClelland & Stewart Inc., 1999.

Duplacey, James. *Hockey's Book of Firsts*. Concord: World Publications Group, 2003.

Fairbridge, Derek and Silas White, ed. *Uncle John's Bathroom Reader: Shoots and Scores*. Vancouver: Raincoast Books, 2005.

Goyens, Chrystian, Allan Turowetz, et al. *The Montréal Forum: Forever Proud (1924–1996)*. Montréal: Les editions Felix, 1996.

Hornby, Lance. *Hockey's Greatest Moments*. Toronto: Key Porter Books Ltd, 2004.

Laberge, Stephan, and Sylvain Bouchard. *Les 100 Plus Grand Hockeyeurs Quebecois de la LNH*. Montréal: Editions Hurtubise, 2005.

Leonetti, Mike. *Canadiens Legends: Montréal's Hockey Heroes*. Vancouver: Raincoast Books, 2003.

Leonetti, Mike. *The Montréal Canadiens Trivia Book: 1909–2005*. Toronto: Harper Collins, 2005.

McFarlane, Brian. *The Best of it Happened in Hockey*. Toronto: Stoddart, 1997.

McKinley, Michael. *Etched in Ice: A Tribute to Hockey's Defining Moments*. Vancouver: Greystone Books, 1998.

Podnieks, Andrew, et al. *Kings of the Ice: A History of World Hockey*. Richmond Hill: NDE Publishing, 2002.

Turowetz, Allan and Goyens, Chrys. *Lions In Winter*. Scarborough: Prentice Hall, 1986.

Weekes, Don. *The Big Book of Hockey Trivia*. Vancouver: Greystone Books, 2005.

National Hockey League Official Rule Book. Toronto: Triumphs Books, 2005.

J. Alexander Poulton

J. Alexander Poulton is a writer, photographer and genuine enthusiast of Canada's national pastime. A resident of Montréal all his life, he has developed a healthy passion for hockey ever since he saw his first Montréal Canadiens game. His favourite memory was meeting the legendary gentleman hockey player Jean Beliveau, who in 1988 towered over the young awe-struck author.

He earned his B.A. in English Literature from McGill University and his graduate diploma in Journalism from Concordia University. He has three other books to his credit: *Canadian Hockey Record Breakers*, *Greatest Moments in Canadian Hockey*, and *Greatest Games of the Stanley Cup*.